GRAVITY

The Universal Force

These and other books are included in the
Encyclopedia of Discovery and Invention
series:

Airplanes: The Lure of Flight
Atoms: Building Blocks of Matter
Computers: Mechanical Minds
Gravity: The Universal Force
Lasers: Humanity's Magic Light
Printing Press: Ideas into Type
Radar: The Silent Detector
Television: Electronic Pictures

GRAVITY
The Universal Force

by DON NARDO

The ENCYCLOPEDIA of
D·I·S·C·O·V·E·R·Y and INVENTION

Lucent Books, P.O. Box 289011 SAN DIEGO, CA 92128-9011

Library of Congress Cataloging-in-Publication Data

Nardo, Don, 1947–
    Gravity, the universal force/by Don Nardo.
      p. cm. — (The Encyclopedia of discovery and invention)
    Includes bibliographical references (p.
    Includes index.
    Summary: Explains the force of gravity, including theories of
gravity and its effects on human life.
      ISBN 1-56006-204-5
    1. Gravity—Juvenile literature. 2. Gravitation—Juvenile
literature. [1. Gravity.] I. Title. II. Series.
QB341.N35   1990
531'.14—dc20   90-6413
                                                              CIP
                                                              AC

Contents

■ ■

Foreword

The belief in progress has been one of the dominant forces in Western Civilization from the Scientific Revolution of the seventeenth century to the present. Embodied in the idea of progress is the conviction that each generation will be better off than the one that preceded it. Eventually, all peoples will benefit from and share in this better world. R. R. Palmer, in his *History of the Modern World,* calls this belief in progress "a kind of nonreligious faith that the conditions of human life" will continually improve as time goes on.

For over a thousand years prior to the seventeenth century, science had progressed little. Inquiry was largely discouraged, and experimentation almost nonexistent. As a result, science became regressive and discovery was ignored. Benjamin Farrington, a historian of science, characterized it this way: "Science had failed to become a real force in the life of society. Instead there had arisen a conception of science as a cycle of liberal studies for a privileged minority. Science ceased to be a means of transforming the conditions of life." In short, had this intellectual climate continued, humanity's future world would have been little more than a clone of its past.

Fortunately, these circumstances were not destined to last. By the seventeenth and eighteenth centuries, Western society was undergoing radical and favorable changes. And the changes that occurred gave rise to the notion that progress was a real force urging civilization forward. Surpluses of consumer goods were replacing substandard living conditions in most of Western Europe. Rigid class systems were giving way to social mobility. In nations like France and the United States, the lofty principles of democracy and popular sovereignty were being painted in broad, gilded strokes over the fading canvasses of monarchy and despotism.

But more significant than these social, economic, and political changes, the new age witnessed a rebirth of science. Centuries of scientific stagnation began crumbling before a spirit of scientific inquiry that spawned undreamed of technological advances. And it was the discoveries and inventions of scores of men and women that fueled these new technologies, dramatically increasing the ability of humankind to control nature—and, many believed, eventually to guide it.

It is a truism of science and technology that the results derived from observation and experimentation are not finalities. They are part of a process. Each discovery is but one piece in a continuum bridging past and present and heralding an extraordinary future. The heroic age of the Scientific Revolution was simply a start. It laid a foundation upon which succeeding generations of imaginative thinkers could build. It kindled the belief that progress is possible as long as there were gifted men and women who would respond to society's needs. When Antonie van Leeuwenhoek observed *Animalcules* (little animals) through his high-powered microscope in 1683, the discovery did not end there. Others followed who would call these "little animals" bacteria and, in time, recognize their role in the process of health and disease. Robert Koch, a German bacteriologist and winner of the Nobel prize in Physiology and Medicine, was one of these men. Koch firmly established that bacteria are responsible for causing infectious diseases. He identified, among others, the causative organisms of anthrax and tuberculosis. Alexander Fleming, another Nobel Laureate, progressed still further in the quest to understand and control bacteria. In 1928, Fleming discovered penicillin, the antibiotic wonder drug. Penicillin, and the generations of antibiotics that succeeded it, have done more to prevent premature death than any other discovery in the history of humankind. And as civilization hastens toward the twenty-first century, most agree that the conquest of van Leeuwenhoek's "little animals" will continue.

The *Encyclopedia of Discovery and Invention* examines those discoveries and inventions that have had a sweeping impact on life and thought in the modern world. Each book explores the ideas that led to the invention or discovery, and, more importantly, how the world changed and continues to change because of it. The series also highlights the people behind the achievements—the unique men and women whose singular genius and rich imagination have altered the lives of everyone. Enhanced by photographs and clearly explained technical drawings, these books are comprehensive examinations of the building blocks of human progress.

GRAVITY

The Universal Force

GRAVITY

Introduction

Anyone who has ever thrown a ball into the air knows that the ball will eventually fall back and hit the ground. Similarly, a person unfortunate enough to tumble from a tall building or cliff will plummet downward until the ground stops the fall. In fact, everything on earth, from people and trees to mountains and oceans, is held tightly to the surface of the planet by a powerful, invisible force. That force is gravity.

Scientists know that gravity is one of four basic forces that hold everything in the universe together. The first three—electromagnetic force and the strong and weak nuclear forces—are actually

... TIMELINE: **GRAVITY**

1 > 2 > 3 > 4 > 5 > 6 > 7 > 8 > 9 > 10 > 11 > 12 > 13 > 14 > 15 >

1 ■ 350 B.C.
Aristotle states the principle of the earth-centered universe.

2 ■ 325 B.C.
Pytheas the Greek studies Atlantic tides.

3 ■ A.D. 140
Ptolemy writes *Almagest*.

4 ■ 1232
First known use of rockets in warfare (China).

5 ■ 1543
Copernicus publishes his concept of the sun-centered universe.

6 ■ 1600
Giordano Bruno is burned at the stake for supporting Copernican system.

7 ■ 1610
Galileo discovers Jupiter's four largest moons.

8 ■ 1618
Kepler publishes his laws of planetary motion.

9 ■ 1666
Newton formulates universal gravitation.

10 ■ 1687
Newton publishes the *Principia*.

11 ■ 1783
Balloons first carry people into the air.

12 ■ 1853
Gliders first carry people.

13 ■ 1895
Tsiolkovsky begins publishing articles on space travel.

14 ■ 1900
First dirigible is launched.

15 ■ 1903
Wright brothers fly the first powered airplane.

much stronger than gravity. However, these forces work only on the subatomic level, that is, the realm of the tiny particles that make up atoms. Though they are millions of times more powerful than gravity, the other forces cannot be felt beyond the scale of a single atom. On the other hand, the pull of gravity can be felt for thousands, even millions of miles. Thus, it is the force of gravity that keeps us cemented firmly to the surface of the earth. It is gravity that holds the sun and planets together, and, in general, guides the motions of all the objects in the known universe.

16 > 17 > 18 > 19 > 20 > 21 > 22 > 23 > 24 > 25 > 26 > 27 >

16 ■ 1905
Einstein publishes the special theory of relativity.

17 ■ 1916
Einstein publishes the general theory of relativity.

18 ■ 1919
Einstein's theory of curved space is confirmed during solar eclipse.

19 ■ 1924
Existence of distant galaxies is confirmed.

20 ■ 1926
Robert Goddard begins launching liquid fuel rockets.

21 ■ 1957
Soviets launch the first satellite, *Sputnik I,* into orbit.

22 ■ 1961
The Soviet Yuri Gagarin becomes the first human to orbit the earth.

23 ■ 1965
Cygnus X-1 is discovered, confirming existence of black holes.

24 ■ 1969
Americans land the first humans on the moon.

25 ■ 1971
Soviets launch the first space laboratory, *Salyut-1,* into orbit.

26 ■ 1979
Voyager satellite flies by Jupiter.

27 ■ 1989
Voyager satellite encounters Neptune.

Searching for Order in the Heavens

Gravity is related to the motions of the heavenly, or celestial, bodies in a fundamental way. Gravity is so important to the underlying structure of the universe that it is impossible to talk about gravity without talking about the celestial bodies themselves. The science that is concerned with the composition and movements of the celestial bodies is called astronomy. In order to find out how people's understanding of gravity developed, it is necessary to consider how the knowledge of astronomy evolved.

Like all sciences, astronomy is concerned with discovering how nature works. This is accomplished by direct observation, measurement, experimentation, and logical deduction. A scientist's chief concern is evidence, that is,

measurable facts that lead to the proof of an idea. Sometimes a scientist wants to explain a certain natural occurrence, or phenomenon. If he or she puts together a number of ideas supported by evidence that seems to explain the phenomenon, the result is a theory. Often the ideas involved in a new theory contradict accepted beliefs. In such cases, the scientist must change or even throw out old theories in favor of the new one, which better matches the evidence. This is part of the scientific method.

But people in ancient and medieval times did not always follow the scientific method. This is because their religious beliefs were so strong. Anything that seemed to go against these beliefs was labeled as heresy, an anti-

Bishops convict a man of heresy for straying from the traditional beliefs of the Church.

religious idea, and condemned. So the development of the science of astronomy, which eventually revealed the true principles behind the motions of the celestial bodies, was a long-drawn-out process.

The Earth-Centered Universe

In ancient times, those who studied astronomy also practiced astrology. Astrology is concerned with how the heavenly bodies influence human beings and their affairs. Today astrology is considered a pseudo, or false, science because there is no evidence to support its claims. But to the the ancients, astrology made sense because it seemed to support the strong religious beliefs of the times.

A medieval astrologer divines the future by studying the stars and planets.

The ancients believed that astrological charts depicted the destinies of medieval states and rulers.

Common to every ancient culture was the basic religious concept that the earth was the center of all things and that the sun, moon, and other heavenly bodies revolved around it. This is known as the geocentric, or earth-centered universe. The earliest, most simplistic beliefs held that the celestial bodies hung by ropes from a solid dome that stretched over the flat earth. According to the geocentric view, a god or gods created the earth and other celestial bodies for the use of human beings, who were the most important creatures in nature.

The planets and other objects in the sky revolved around human beings on earth. Because of this, it seemed only logical that these objects must have some influence on people's lives. For instance, a common astrological belief held that the position of the sun in the sky at the time of a person's birth decided whether that person would be a ruler or a slave. The position of the sun also determined aspects of personality, such as whether a person would be kind or cruel.

So astrology and religious beliefs dictated what people were supposed to believe about the heavens. All observations of the celestial sphere were made to fit neatly into the accepted geocentric world concept. These observations

A map depicts the ancient belief that the Earth was the center of the universe. The Church believed that this order was created by God.

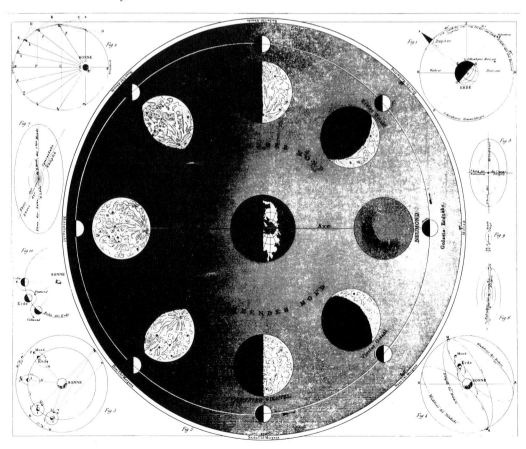

included the motions of the planets, now known to be directed by gravity. Any new theories that strayed from traditional beliefs were frowned upon or suppressed.

The prevailing beliefs about the forces and motions of the universe were formally stated about the year 350 B.C. by the Greek philosopher Aristotle. His geocentric view of the universe profoundly influenced scholars of the ancient and medieval worlds. It became the model accepted and endorsed by the major religions.

Aristotle tried to explain the various observed natural phenomena now known to be caused by gravity. For instance, he knew that something held the celestial bodies in their orbits above the earth. He envisioned a series of invisible spheres, or shells, that ran through the sky. Each planet or other heavenly body was encased in its own sphere and did not come into contact with other bodies. Aristotle also considered the phenomenon of earth-based gravity. He, like everyone else, noticed that objects thrown into the air fell back to the ground. But he tended to take this everyday occurrence for granted. He did not connect it with the motions of the celestial bodies. Aristotle did not make any direct experiments with falling objects to see *how* they fell and at what speeds. Instead, he relied on assumption

The ideas of the Greek philosopher Aristotle had a prevailing influence on medieval and later thought.

and concluded that heavier objects fell faster than lighter ones. This and most of his other statements about the forces of nature turned out to be incorrect. But nearly eighteen hundred years would pass before scientists seriously began to question the views of the universe set down by Aristotle and perpetuated by organized religion.

About five centuries after Aristotle, another Greek, Ptolemy, took Aristotle's writings, along with those of other Greek thinkers, and incorporated them into a large volume of astronomical knowledge. The volume, called

The series of invisible spheres envisioned by Aristotle. He believed that such spheres encased and upheld all celestial bodies.

Almagest, appeared about the year A.D. 140 in Alexandria, Egypt, where a colony of Greek scientists, including Ptolemy, lived and worked. Ptolemy supported Aristotle's views. Like Aristotle, Ptolemy recognized that some force must account for the motions of the heavenly bodies. But instead of offering a new explanation, Ptolemy fell back on the idea of invisible spheres.

Ptolemy also postulated, or proposed, that some force must hold objects to the surface of the earth. He did not, however, give the force a name. Like Aristotle, he did not connect this force with the movements of the planets. In addition, he insisted that the sun, planets, and other celestial bodies moved in circles. This was because a circle is a "perfect" geometrical shape.

A chart depicts Ptolemy's geocentric cosmology. Like Aristotle, he believed that all celestial bodies moved in circles around the earth.

The Greek astronomer Ptolemy supported many of Aristotle's beliefs. He is well-known for his book Almagest, *in which he incorporated the astronomical views of mathematicians, geographers, and astronomers.* Almagest *appeared in the year A.D. 140.*

Since it was assumed that God had set the heavenly bodies in motion, it was unthinkable to suppose that the Creator would have done so in any manner less than perfect. Once again, unsupported assumptions, rather than theories supported by evidence, ruled the day.

But not all ancient scholars felt bound by the chains of Aristotelian dogma. For instance, a few dared to suggest that, although the earth appeared to be flat, it was in fact a sphere. This seemingly outrageous notion was advanced by the Greek scientists Aristarchus of Samos and Eratosthenes. They further proposed that the sun, not the earth, was the center of the universe. This was the first appearance of

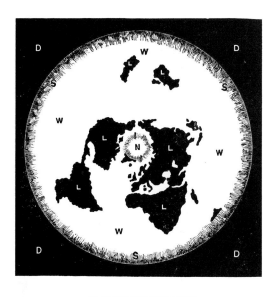

SECTIONAL VIEW OF EARTH'S SURFACE.

Ancient scientists believed the Earth was flat as shown here. The Greek scientists Aristarchus and Eratosthenes were among the first to suggest that this may not be the case.

the heliocentric, or sun-centered, theory of the heavens. Unlike Aristotle, Aristarchus and Eratosthenes used direct experimentation to test their ideas. For instance, Eratosthenes used observations of shadows cast by sticks and simple geometry to calculate the circumference of the earth rather accurately. But Eratosthenes' ideas received little attention and were generally ridiculed in accepted "scientific" circles. Within a few generations, these ideas were forgotten. More than a dozen centuries passed before they resurfaced to challenge traditional beliefs.

The Copernican Revolution

The great champion of the heliocentric theory was the Polish astronomer Nicolaus Copernicus. Copernicus insisted that the earth was one of the planets that moved around the sun. He also used mathematics to find the approximate distances of the sun and planets. These distances were far greater than anyone had yet imagined. Naturally, the Christian Church objected to Copernicus' theory. For instance, the religious leader Martin Luther rejected the idea that the earth moves. He based his argument on the "evidence" of the Bible. God, said Luther, had commanded the sun to stand still for Joshua; therefore, it was the sun that moved, not the earth.

Sixteenth-century astronomers use sticks to cast shadows. These experiments provided data for the study of planetary movement.

PTOLEMY'S GEOCENTRIC UNIVERSE

COPERNICAN HELIOCENTRIC SOLAR SYSTEM

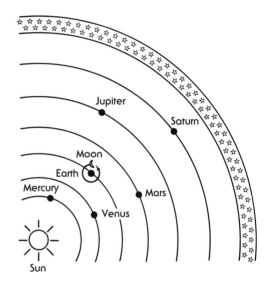

Ptolemy's idea of a geocentric, or Earth-centered universe was the most widely accepted view of the universe until the middle of the seventeenth century. It explained what people thought they saw with their own eyes. From the Earth, it appears that the sun, moon, planets, and stars revolve around the Earth.

The first serious challenge to the Ptolemaic system came in the mid-1500s. That is when Copernicus proposed his heliocentric, or sun-centered, system. Copernicus explained that the sun and planets only appear to revolve around the Earth because the Earth is constantly turning like a top. As the Earth spins from west to east, it makes the sun and planets look like they are moving around the Earth in the opposite direction.

Copernicus set down his ideas in a volume called *De Revolutionibus (On the Revolutions)*. This volume was published in 1543, the year of his death. Although he laid the groundwork for modern astronomy, not all of his ideas were correct. A deeply religious person, he still clung to the idea that God must have made the planets move in perfect circles. Copernicus believed that the sun exerted some kind of force that held the planets in place. But, like his ancient predecessors, he failed to see the connection between planetary movements and falling objects. The real nature of gravity still lay hidden from science.

Later, in 1616, the Catholic Church placed *De Revolutionibus* on its list of forbidden books until it was "properly censored" by church scholars. The Church still insisted that, since God had made everything in nature, people should

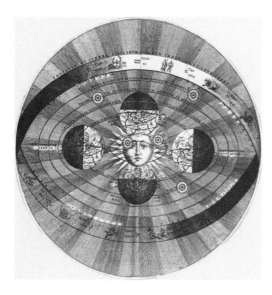

A diagram illustrates the theories of Nicolaus Copernicus, who insisted that all celestial bodies orbit the sun.

not question how nature works. To do so, said church leaders, was the same as questioning whether or not God exists. Such thinking was considered a threat, not only to God, but also to the Church itself, which represented God in earthly matters. So strong was religion's hold on people's minds that scientists who proposed radical ideas often risked public ridicule, expulsion from the Church, or even death.

Such was the case of Giordano Bruno, a brilliant Italian priest whose proposals immediately aroused the ire of the Catholic Church. Bruno took Copernicus' ideas a step further and declared that the stars were actually other suns. Each of these suns, claimed Bruno, had its own system of planets, with each planet held in place by a natural force. He did not name this force, which we now call gravity. But Bruno concluded that the force that held planets to other stars was the same force that held the sun and the mem-

bers of its own family together. He also suggested that some of the planets revolving around distant stars might harbor animals and people. For this "dangerous" heresy, the Church burned Bruno at the stake in the year 1600.

Only a few years after the death of Bruno, the Church once more found itself battling against the heliocentric theory. This time, the spokesman for science was the formidable Italian scholar, Galileo Galilei. Although Galileo did not invent the telescope (then called the optick tube), he was the first person to use the new device to study astronomy. In 1610, he aimed his telescope at the planet Jupiter and immediately noticed four bright points of light near the planet. By observing Jupiter over the course of several

German religious leader Martin Luther objected to Copernicus' heliocentric theory. He often quoted biblical passages to support his belief that man was at the center of the universe.

In the sixteenth century, Copernicus' dissatisfaction with the geocentric theory led him to formulate the heliocentric, or sun-centered, theory of the universe.

A drawing depicts God creating the universe. The Catholic Church refused to embrace any radical ideas that deviated from their view of God as the creator of all things.

In the year 1600, the Italian priest Giordano Bruno was burned at the stake for advocating the Copernican hypothesis and stating that there may be other life in the universe.

nights, Galileo found that the bright points appeared to circle the planet. The scientist had discovered four moons revolving around Jupiter. This was a find of tremendous importance at the time for three reason. First, the fact that four bodies revolved around Jupiter proved that all celestial objects did *not* revolve around Earth. Second, Jupiter seemed able to exert a force to hold its satellites in place, just as the sun exerted a force to hold Jupiter itself in place. This suggested that planets too might give off invisible forces. Third, the discovery of Jupiter's moons showed that Aristotle and Ptolemy were not infallible, which was the official claim of the Church. This helped open the door to other scientific discoveries, including those concerning gravity.

Galileo became a staunch proponent of the Copernican, heliocentric

Galileo Galilei aims the newly developed telescope into the heavens. In 1610, Galileo proved that not all celestial bodies revolved around the earth.

theory. Other scientists began to listen to him, and church leaders became worried. In 1615, the Catholic Church denounced Galileo and warned him against teaching the Copernican theory. However, the scientist ignored the warning and continued with his studies and experiments.

Galileo reasoned that, since Aristotle had been wrong to think the earth was the center of the universe, he might also have been wrong about other things. Galileo decided to test Aristotle's assumption that heavier objects fall faster than lighter ones. There is no evidence to support the popular fable that claims Galileo dropped objects of different weights off the Leaning Tower of Pisa. It is more likely that he rolled iron balls down inclined planes. In any case, his was the first recorded scientific experiment designed to test and measure the force of gravity.

Galileo's experiment clearly showed that objects of different weights fall a given distance in the same amount of time (excluding the effects of air resistance). Galileo also noted that objects accelerate, or move faster and faster, as they fall downward. In addition, during his research, Galileo theorized that

once a celestial body was in motion, no extra force was needed to keep it going. He thought that it should continue moving in a straight line. However, the planets obviously did not move in straight lines. The fact that Earth did not fly away from the sun, or Jupiter's moons escape from Jupiter suggested that some powerful force must be hold-

Italian physicist Galileo Galilei discovered the laws of gravity and recorded many scientific experiments.

A drawing depicts Aristotle's assumption that heavier objects fall faster than lighter ones. Galileo Galilei discovered that objects of different weight fall at the same speed.

and moons in their orbits. He and the other scientists of his day still saw the two forces as separate and unrelated.

Eventually, the Church caught up with Galileo. He had to submit to a humiliating trial. During this trial, he was forced to publicly renounce the scientific theories he had devoted his life to explaining. Found guilty of heresy, he was sentenced to house arrest, under which, a few years later, he died.

The Church's victory over Galileo was both hollow and short-lived. Other scientists continued to advance the Copernican system. Their application of mathematics and careful experimentation increasingly supported the ideas of the heliocentric theory. But there was still a major problem with the theory. The stumbling block concerned the motions of the planets around the sun. The orbits of these bodies could be roughly calculated and predicted, but never precisely determined. For some reason, the mathematical models of the circular planetary orbits never completely matched the actual ob-

ing these bodies in their orbits. But even Galileo was not able to establish the correlation between the force that attracted objects to the earth's surface and the force that kept the planets

Galileo as he was forced to renounce his scientific theories before the Church.

served motions of the planets. Until completely accurate predictions could be made, the Church and other opponents of the heliocentric system would have grounds to discredit the theory.

The Motions of the Planets Explained

In 1600, the year Bruno was executed, a young German mathematician named Johannes Kepler traveled to Prague, Czechoslovakia. His mission was to assist the renowned Danish astronomer Tycho Brahe. Brahe had compiled a huge mass of observational data on the motions of the celestial bodies. Kepler immediately recognized that Brahe's data was much more accurate than the information handed down from ancient and medieval schol-

Danish astronomer Tycho Brahe works in his laboratory. His accurate data inspired Johannes Kepler to formulate the three laws of motion.

In the early seventeenth century, German mathematician Johannes Kepler observed that planets follow elliptical paths rather than circular ones.

ars. Most astronomers of Kepler's day still used this ancient information. Soon after Kepler joined Brahe, the older man died, leaving Kepler a great amount of astronomical data. Kepler quickly began carrying out detailed calculations based on the data.

At first, Kepler tried to make Brahe's observations fit the "perfect" circles that everyone still assumed constituted the orbits of the heavenly bodies. But no matter how hard he tried, Kepler's figures would not match the observed planetary motions. After years of frustration, he finally hit upon what seemed to him a disturbing notion. Perhaps the planets did not move in circular orbits after all. If the orbits were shaped like imperfect ovals instead, his mathematical calculations would precisely match Brahe's observational data.

The idea of imperfect oval orbits also mathematically supported the theory that the sun itself exerted a force that held the planets in place. But how would this affect the image of the Creator, who was supposed to have made only perfect things? Kepler thought it over. He reasoned that, during Creation, God might have endowed the sun and planets with the ability to exert forces. Since the sun was only an object, it would not be expected to perform perfectly. This seemed to explain how God could create a universe in which some things were imperfect. Kepler recognized other examples. The earth and human beings were far from perfect, yet God had created them. Moreover, the image of the moon as seen through a telescope revealed a surface pitted by craters and cracks. And the sun's image was periodically marred by black sunspots. So the moon and sun were not perfect either. Clearly, thought Kepler, the orbits of the celestial bodies did not have to be perfect.

Thus Kepler realized that he and the scientists who had preceded him had all deluded themselves about the shape of the planetary orbits. The orbits were ellipses, not circles. An ellipse is an oval, something like the shape of an egg. A line drawn through the middle of the long part of the ellipse is called the major axis. Along the major axis lie two off-centered points called the foci (one is called a focus) that share a mathematical relationship with any given point on the ellipse. After much careful calculation, Kepler realized that the "planets orbit the sun in

The cratered surface of the moon proves that not all things are perfect. Spurred on by this observation, Johannes Kepler reasoned that planetary orbits could be imperfect—elliptical rather than circular—as well.

ellipses, with the sun at one focus." He called this his first law of planetary motion. This law had one immediate and significant implication. Since the sun did not rest at the center of Earth's orbit, sometimes Earth was closer to the sun than it was at other times. Thus the distance between Earth and sun changed slightly from season to season.

Kepler went on to formulate two other laws of motion. Both of these laws, like his first, were related to how the sun's gravity affects the planets and their motions. But Kepler, like the other scientists of his day, did not yet understand the workings of gravity. He formulated the laws of motion based strictly on observations of planetary movements. His second law concerns the speed at which the planets move in their orbits. When a planet is farthest from the sun, it moves slowly. When the planet reaches its closest point to the sun, on the other side of the elliptical orbit, it moves much more quickly.

Kepler's third law of motion relates a planet's period (the amount of time it takes to orbit the sun) to its distance from the sun. A planet like Saturn, which is relatively far from the sun, has a much larger orbit than Venus, which is relatively close to the sun. Because Saturn's orbit is larger, Saturn moves at a slower velocity (speed) than Venus. The farther away a planet is from the sun, the slower it moves and the longer is its period.

Kepler published his three laws between 1609 and 1618. He showed that they described more than just the orbits of the planets. The moon's orbit about Earth, and the way Jupiter's moons orbited Jupiter could be explained and predicted by Kepler's three laws. Also, the orbit of every comet and asteroid could be explained and predicted using these laws.

But Kepler was not content to merely explain how the celestial bodies moved. He wanted to discover *why* they moved as they did. Like Galileo, he knew that some invisible force must be holding the sun and planets together. Otherwise, the forward motion of the planets themselves would send them careening off into space.

Eventually, Kepler suggested that magnetism was the force holding the members of the solar system together. "My aim," he said, "is to show that . . . all the manifold movements are carried out by means of a single, quite simple magnetic force." Kepler's choice of magnetism was ultimately shown to be incorrect. However, his prediction that one simple, underlying force governed the movements of the heavenly bodies turned out be accurate. In addition, Kepler had done something never before attempted in science. In his day, magnetism was a physical force that people thought existed only on Earth. Kepler tried to connect this earth-based force with the forces in the heavens.

Until the day he died, Kepler never doubted that the hand of the Creator had shaped the heavens. And he still clung to the belief that the various celestial spheres had some kind of influence over people's lives. Yet he also correctly maintained that the planets were unique worlds. Amazingly, he also prophesied space travel to the moon and beyond. His mathematical calculations sounded the death knell for the Church's suppression of scientific knowledge. Kepler helped open the way for the advance of modern astronomy, including the eventual explanation of gravity.

KEPLER'S LAWS

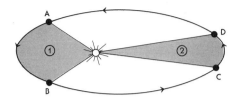

Around 1600, Johannes Kepler meticulously charted the positions of the planets at different times. He discovered that the path of a planet around the sun is not a perfect circle but an ellipse, or oval shape. The sun is not at the center of this ellipse. Rather, it is at a special point to one side of the center known as a focus point. This is known as Kepler's First Law of Motion.

Kepler also noticed that a planet does not always travel at the same speed. It moves fastest when it is nearest the sun, and it moves slowest when it is farthest from the sun. Kepler learned that the exact distance a planet travels during any period of time can be predicted. His Second Law of Motion states that an imaginary line from the sun to a planet always sweeps over equal areas in the planet's orbit in equal times. For example, if area 1 and area 2 in the orbit drawn above are equal, then the planet will travel from A to B in the same amount of time as it takes to travel from C to D.

Kepler's discoveries did little to change the world during his own lifetime. As is the case with many great thinkers, his work did not have a great impact on society until after his death. But that impact was not long in coming. Twelve years after Kepler's death, a child was born in the tiny village of Woolsthorpe in England. As the boy grew, his family and teachers marveled at his quick mind and hearty appetite for knowledge. Within a few short years, he would pick up where Kepler had left off. He would at last provide humanity with the answer to the riddle of what keeps the planets in their courses. And, unlike Kepler, he would have the benefit of watching his own discoveries forever change the way people see the universe and their place within it.

Solving the Riddle of the Mystery Force

In 1666, Johannes Kepler had been dead for thirty-six years. During that year, an outbreak of plague forced many students attending Cambridge University in England to return home for the winter. However, one twenty-three-year-old undergraduate kept himself busy. He spent the winter working out formulas and ideas that would lay much of the groundwork for modern science. In that single season, he invented the mathematical system of calculus. He also discovered the fundamental nature of light. In addition, he devised a monumental theory explaining how gravity holds the universe together. This remarkable young man was Isaac Newton. Many have called him the greatest scientific genius who ever lived. Astonished at how much Newton had accomplished in a single year, his teachers asked him how he had made

his discoveries. Newton modestly replied, "By thinking upon them."

Defining Gravity

Since childhood, Newton had been fascinated by the beauty and mathematical symmetry of the Copernican system. He had taken a special interest in the hypothetical force that held the planets and other celestial bodies in their orbits. Like Galileo and Kepler, Newton recognized that a body in motion should continue to move along in a straight line unless something stops it. He also suggested that a body at rest, or standing still, should stay at rest unless something gets it moving. Newton called this tendency of bodies to keep moving or stay at rest inertia. He formally coined the law of inertia as fol-

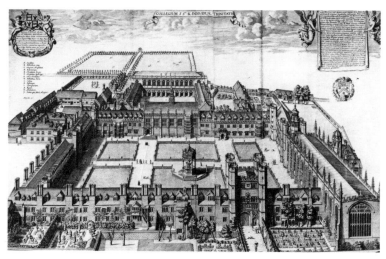

A picture depicts Cambridge University in England, where Isaac Newton invented calculus and formulated important theories.

The great philosopher and mathematician Isaac Newton greatly influenced modern scientific thought with his gravitational theories and mathematical formulas.

fly out of its orbit if some other force were not pulling the planet toward the sun. And the pull of that force must be exactly equal to the strength of Earth's inertia. If the pull of the force was greater than Earth's inertia, the planet would be drawn inward and plunge into the sun. In short, the two forces must balance. They must, in a sense, cancel each other out, allowing Earth to remain in the same orbit year after year.

lows: "A body at rest will stay at rest, and a body in motion will stay in motion, unless either body is acted upon by some outside force."

Like his predecessors, Newton reasoned that inertia would cause Earth to

Newton likened the situation to a ball at the end of a string being whirled around by a person's hand. The ball represents Earth or some other orbiting celestial body, and the person's hand is the sun. The initial push the person exerts to put the ball in motion introduces inertia. That push should be enough to make the ball fly away into the air. But it does not. The string, representing the mystery force that counteracts the effect of inertia, holds the ball in place. Obviously, if the string is suddenly cut, the ball will go flying off into the air. Similarly, if the sun's gravity were suddenly eliminated, Earth

A drawing illustrates Isaac Newton's theory that some force counteracts the Earth's inertia. In this example, the ball represents a planet and the boy's hand is the sun. The string is the mystery force that Newton studied. Once the ball is in motion, the string keeps the ball from flying off into the air, similar to the way that gravity keeps the planets from flying off into space.

Isaac Newton spent a lot of time thinking about the laws of the universe. As he watches an apple fall from a tree, Newton postulates that earth-based gravity and the mystery force in the heavens are the same.

would go flying off into space. Thus, deduced Newton, the mystery force, acting like millions of invisible strings, must exist throughout the known universe. Otherwise, the planets and moons would fly around randomly, and the heavens would be in a state of chaos.

But what was this mystery force that held the heavenly bodies in place? Newton claims to have gotten a clue to the nature of the force from watching an apple fall from a tree. Like Galileo and other scholars, Newton knew that objects on Earth were drawn toward the center of the planet by some unknown power. Newton's great contribution was to relate this Earth-based power, which he called gravity, to the heavenly bodies. Newton's clue that gravity was a property of the heavenly bodies, as well as of Earth, was the concept of distance.

Everyone before Newton thought that the celestial bodies were too far away to be affected by earthly forces. Newton

pointed out that, whether in the deepest mines or on the highest mountain peaks, objects still fell downward. Thus gravity pulled at things over distances of at least thousands of feet. Maybe it worked over even greater distances.

The fall of the apple somehow reminded Newton of the moon. The apple fell toward the center of the Earth. Perhaps, reasoned Newton, the celestial mystery force that held the moon in place would also cause it to fall if not for the opposing force of inertia. It seemed logical to Newton that Earth-based gravity and the mystery force were the same. Therefore, the same force that held the apple and Newton himself to the ground also held the moon to the Earth. In addition, it held the Earth to the sun, and kept all the other planets and celestial bodies in their places. This force, then, must be universal. So Newton called his explanation of the force the law of universal gravitation.

The Formula for Gravitation

Newton's conclusion was that every piece of matter in the universe, no matter how big or how small, attracts every other piece of matter. He found that the strength of this gravitational force could be demonstrated by a simple formula. To begin with, said Newton, the force of gravity is related to mass. This is the amount of matter contained in a given physical body. Newton explained that a small body like a chair has very little mass. It therefore exerts very little gravitational force—certainly not enough to attract nearby objects. On the other hand, a large body like a planet has a tremendous amount of mass. So, it exerts a great deal of gravitational force and is able to hold down pebbles, rocks, mountains, and even moons.

The force of gravity, said Newton, is also related to distance. The farther two objects are from each other, the less gravitational force each exerts on the other. Because they attract each other less, they are said to have a smaller force of attraction. Conversely, the closer the objects are, the stronger the pull of gravity between them and the larger their force of attraction. Thus, for example, Earth easily holds in orbit the moon, which is relatively near. However, it has no important gravitational effect on Mars, which is much farther away.

Newton expressed his formula in the following way: the force of attraction (f) between any two objects is related to the masses ($m1$ and $m2$) of the objects and also to the distance (d) between the objects. Newton also discovered and calculated the value of a special figure that is present in the formula, no matter which objects are involved. Because this figure always stays the same, or remains constant, he called it the gravitational constant (G) using the formula

$$f = G \frac{m_1 \times m_2}{d^2}$$

Newton demonstrated that the force of attraction between any bodies in the universe could be easily calculated.

In addition, the mass of a body could be found, providing that there was another large body orbiting it and that the distance to the bodies was known. For instance, the masses of the Earth and moon could be found, since the distance between these bodies was known. Using Newton's formula, scientists deduced that the Earth is eighty-one times more massive than the moon. In other words, if the Earth were placed on one side of a giant scale, eighty-one bodies having the mass of the moon would have to be placed on the other side of the scale for balance.

Finding the Masses of the Planets

Scientists have used Newton's gravitational formula to discover the masses of other celestial bodies. For instance, once the mass of the Earth-moon system was known, the mass of the sun could be worked out; since the distance from Earth to the sun was known. The sun's mass turned out to be about 333,400 times the mass of Earth. That means that 333,400 Earths would be needed on the imaginary scale to balance out the sun. That the sun has such a huge mass did not surprise many scientists. They already

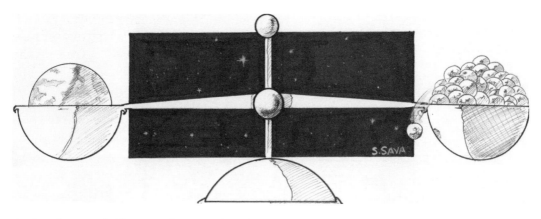

An imaginary scale illustrates the mass of Earth. It would take the mass of eighty-one moons to balance out the weight of the Earth.

knew the sun was an enormous body. It appeared so large in Earth's sky, even at a distance of ninety-three million miles.

After the sun's mass was known, finding the masses of the other planets became comparatively easy. Great extremes in the masses of the planets were discovered. For instance, Mercury, the planets closest to the sun, was found to be only one-sixth as massive as Earth. Jupiter, the largest planet in the solar system, has a mass some 318 times that of Earth. The masses of Jupiter's four largest moons were also worked out. Some scientists were surprised to learn that three of the four are more massive than Earth's moon. The largest, Ganymede, has about two-and-a-half times the mass of Earth's moon, and Io and Callisto have one-and-a-half times that mass. Only Europa is smaller, having a bit more than half of the mass of Earth's moon.

Callistro is one of the moons of Jupiter, the largest planet in the solar system. Its mass is one-and-a-half times that of the Earth's moon.

The mass of Europa, another of Jupiter's moons, is slightly more than half of the mass of Earth's moon.

Expanding on Universal Gravitation

Scientists also found that Newton's theory of universal gravitation could be used as a springboard into other formulas and calculations about the celestial bodies. For instance, consider Kepler's laws of planetary motion. Newton had studied them and later admitted that they had given him the inspiration for his theory of gravitation. Newton showed that these same laws could be mathematically derived from his own gravitation formula. Kepler found the laws *directly*, by observing the motions of the planets. Newton demonstrated the laws *indirectly*, through his gravitation formula. The two men had taken different paths to the same universal truths.

Scientists also learned to use Newton's theory of gravitation to study the strength of the pull of gravity at the surfaces of Earth and other heavenly bodies. Obviously, the more massive the body, the more strongly it holds objects to its surface. Scientists in Newton's day often used the example of a cannonball to show how objects reacted to the pull of gravity. When a ball was fired into the air, it followed a curved path upward. It reached a maximum altitude, then fell back in a continuation of the curved path. When a larger, more powerful cannon was used, the ball traveled faster and reached a higher maximum altitude. Clearly, the strength of gravity's pull on a body was directly related to how fast the body was moving. The faster the speed, the less strongly gravity pulled.

Newton also showed that the force of gravity decreases with distance. There-fore the higher the altitude attained by a cannonball, the less strongly gravity will pull on the ball. Theoretically then, if a ball can be propelled fast enough and high enough, the pull on Earth's gravity will become so small, that the ball will no longer fall back to the planet's surface. One of two things can then happen. First, the inertia of the ball, its tendency to keep on moving, might equal the pull of gravity upon it. In that case, it will move neither up nor down. Instead, it will go into orbit around Earth, becoming an artificial satellite of the planet. The moon, a natural satellite, orbits Earth for the same reason. The moon's inertia and the pull of Earth's gravity on the moon are in balance. As a second possibility, the inertia of the cannonball might exceed the pull of gravity upon it, in which case the ball will move away from Earth, never to return.

In both of these cases, the ball will have attained a speed high enough to allow it to escape from Earth. Scientists call that speed the escape velocity. As it turns out, Earth's escape velocity is about 7 miles per second (miles/sec). That means that any object traveling less than 7 miles/sec will eventually fall back to Earth. And any object traveling 7 miles/sec or faster will either go into orbit or fly off into space.

From Newton's computations, it follows that bodies of different masses will have different escape velocities. For example, a body more massive than Earth will have a higher escape velocity. A cannonball fired from the surface of a planet the size of Jupiter will be pulled downward much more strongly than it would be on Earth. This is because the more massive planet would

ESCAPE VELOCITY

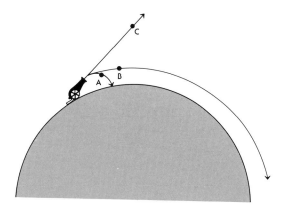

The Earth's escape velocity is about 7 miles per second. If you fire a cannonball into the air and it does not reach the speed of 7 miles per second, it will eventually fall back to the Earth (A).

The faster you can make the cannonball travel, the higher and farther it can travel before falling to the Earth. If you had a powerful enough cannon to make a cannonball go 7 miles per second, it would never come down. Instead, it would stay in orbit around the Earth (B).

Finally, if you had such a powerful cannon that the cannonball's speed exceeded the escape velocity, it would fly off the Earth and into space (C).

have a more powerful gravitational pull. Consequently, the ball will need to attain a much higher velocity to escape the larger planet. The escape velocity of Jupiter is about 38 miles/sec, more than five times that of Earth.

Although Jupiter is the largest planet, its escape velocity is by no means the highest in the solar system. The sun itself is so massive that its escape velocity is 385 miles/sec—ten times that of Jupiter. Firing a cannonball off the sun would be a mighty feat. (Of course, such a feat could never actually be attempted. The sun has no solid surface on which to rest a cannon. Also, both cannon and cannonball would vaporize in a fraction of a second because of the sun's enormous heat.)

By contrast, bodies less massive than Earth have lower escape velocities. To escape from Mars, a cannonball would have to travel only a bit more than 3 miles/sec. The ball would have an even easier time getting away from the moon, which has an escape velocity of about 1.5 miles/sec. The escape velocity of the moon may have seemed a figure of trivial importance in Newton's day. No one at that time dreamed it would ever have a practical application. But knowing that figure made it possible for the astronauts of Apollo 11 to return to Earth after the first moon landing in 1969. Neither that nor any other space flight could have occurred without Newton's law of universal gravitation.

Using Isaac Newton's gravitational formula, scientists are able to discover the mass of the Earth in relation to other planets. For example, the sun's mass is 333,400 times that of Earth, shown here.

A Revolution in Science and Thought

The beauty of Newton's theory is that it explains so much. It can be used to calculate the mass of practically any celestial body. It can also be used to demonstrate the laws of planetary motion and to measure the force of gravity exerted between any two objects. The theory also explains the motions of objects on the Earth and the actions of the tides, which, Newton showed, result from the gravitational attractions of the sun and moon. Newton eventually set down the details of universal gravitation in a volume entitled *Mathematical Principles of Natural Philosophy.* Commonly called the *Principia,* this volume was published in 1687. Wrote Newton in the book's opening, "I now demon-strate the frame of the system of the world."

The effects of the *Principia* on the scientific world were immediate and far-reaching. The book laid the foundation for the entire development of modern science, especially for the discipline of astronomy. During the following two centuries, many theories were advanced about the origin and nature of the universe. All of these theories began with Newton's ideas on universal gravitation. Newton demonstrated that a single mathematical law can explain the motions of all the bodies in nature. He showed that the forces behind those motions are consistent throughout the known universe. Earth is not a special case, set apart from the rest of the celestial bodies, as had been previously thought. Instead, Earth obeys the same natural laws as the other planets. With Newton's theory, there is order and predictability in the heavens.

Many people believe that Isaac Newton possessed the greatest scientific mind in history.

But there were those who resisted the notion that Earth was just one more tiny globe orbiting in a huge, nearly empty cosmos. Religious leaders feared the public's acceptance of a universe in which people were no longer the center of creation. But the power the Church had used to suppress Bruno, Galileo, and others now paled before a greater power—the mathematical truth of natural law as revealed by Newton. As Newton's new order took hold of the minds of men and women, the old order perpetuated by the Church began to lose credibility.

It was not that people lost faith in God. Newton himself remained a devout Christian all his life. What changed was the way human beings saw themselves and their place in the universe. The revolution begun by Copernicus and completed by Newton did more than introduce new knowledge. It also instilled in people the belief that they possessed the power to understand how the universe works. In ancient and medieval times, this power had been thought to be solely the province of God. After Newton, scientists went forth with a new confidence in their own abilities to meet the challenge of fathoming nature's secrets.

In the post-Newton age, science no longer worked on assumptions and dogmatic traditions. The worth of new ideas and theories was now judged on the basis of evidence. If old beliefs did not stand up to the measure of natural laws, the beliefs, not the laws, had to bend. The Church too had to bend. It had to concede that God did not make people the center of all things. Instead, human beings occupy an insignificant speck in a universe of immense proportions. Lamented one of the devout, "I

The English writer Alexander Pope applauded Newton's quest for scientific knowledge and ridiculed the Church's dogmatic traditions.

am terrified by the eternal silence of these infinite spaces."

But many argued that the status of humanity in nature's scheme had not been lowered by Newton's insights. To the contrary, men and women had been raised up. Before, they had been humble creatures, powerless before and obedient to the authority of the Church. Now they were dignified, intelligent beings, able to understand their world and control their own destinies. People seemed suddenly invigorated by a bold new spirit. Whole new vistas of knowledge lay open for human beings to explore and conquer. As writer Alexander Pope put it, "Nature and nature's laws lay hid in night; God said 'Let Newton be,' and all was light."

Living with Gravity on Earth

Newton showed how gravity controls the movements of all the celestial bodies. But such work as calculating the orbits and masses of Jupiter's moons remained primarily a concern of astronomers. The common person was interested in gravity only insofar as it affected everyday life. Newton's revelations had not changed one basic fact of gravity on Earth—a person who fell from a great height faced injury or death.

But the effects on civilization of Newton's gravitational discoveries, if not immediately obvious, were nevertheless profound. To begin with, the theory of universal gravitation had at last explained the workings of one of the most common, yet mysterious of earthly phenomena—the tides.

Gravity and Earth's Oceans

Many people in the ancient world were not familiar with the tides. That was because many of the early civilizations grew up around the Mediterranean Sea, which is nearly tideless. In time, however, Mediterranean explorers began to venture out along the coastlines of the open oceans. There they noticed that the water climbed up onto the shore, then retreated, in a twice-a-day cycle.

One explorer who was particularly fascinated by the action of the tides was a Greek, Pytheas of Massalia, who sailed out into the Atlantic Ocean about the year 325 B.C. Pytheas noticed that the monthly variations in the rise and fall

A fishing boat floats in the Atlantic Ocean at dawn. In 325 B.C., the Greek explorer Pytheas sailed these same waters and noticed a correlation between the phases of the moon and water level.

The tide rolls onto the coast of Oregon. Tidal motions are primarily detectable in water because it is less rigid than land.

of the waters seemed to match the phases of the moon. So he concluded that the moon somehow caused the tides. Although a few later Greek astronomers agreed with this conclusion, most ancient and medieval scholars rejected the idea.

Even when the great mathematician Johannes Kepler professed a belief in moon-generated tides, other scientists refused to accept such a notion. Galileo himself thought the idea was astrological nonsense. He insisted that the tides were the result of Earth's oceans sloshing back and forth as the planet rotated.

Both Pytheas and Kepler were finally vindicated by Newton, who showed that the moon exerts a gravitational pull on the oceans and thereby causes the tides. Newton explained the occurrence of two tides each day in the following manner: the moon pulls on the surface of the Earth, creating bulges on opposite sides. As the Earth rotates, a given point on its surface moves completely around once in twenty-four hours. Since there are two tidal bulges,

the point passes through one of the bulges every twelve hours. The solid ground yields so little to the tug of gravity that its effects are barely noticeable. But water is far less rigid than the land masses. As the oceans pass through each bulge, they swell and contract accordingly. This generates waves and causes water to creep up and down the edges of the land. Since the oceans pass through two bulges in a twenty-four-hour period, there are two tides in a day. Newton showed that the sun's gravity causes tides too, although to a lesser degree than the gravity of the moon. The sun produces ocean bulges too, but they are quite small.

Newton's calculations also explain why tides at different times of the year vary in intensity. For instance, the abnormally high spring tides occur at times of new moon and full moon. At these times, the moon and sun are lined up in such a way that the bulges in the oceans produced by the moon and sun coincide. The bulges add to each other and cause a larger-than-nor-

MOON'S GRAVITY CAUSES TIDAL BULGES

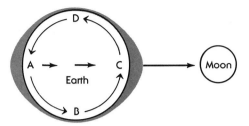

As the Earth rotates, only a portion of its surface faces the moon at any one time. Since this area of the Earth is about 4,000 miles closer to the moon than the center of the Earth is, it is pulled more strongly by the moon's gravity. It is strong enough to pull sea water from the Earth's oceans into a bulge in the area facing the moon (C). This bulge creates a high tide on the ocean shores in this area.

There is another bulge on the side away from the moon (A). That is because the moon's gravity pulls more strongly on the middle of the Earth than it does on the far side. This pulls the Earth a few inches away from the oceans on the far side, causing the ocean water to flow into a bulge and create a high tide.

As the Earth rotates, another part of its surface faces the moon. When Area B reaches the point where C is now shown, it will have high tides. As the day goes on, Area C will reach the point farthest from the moon and have its second high tide of the day. Because the moon is also moving, it takes twenty-five hours to complete a full cycle of two high tides and two low tides.

---

mal difference between high and low tides.

Newton's theory made it possible to predict the tides at any spot on the globe with great precision and reliability. Such predictions could also be made far into the future. This knowledge aided in the expansion of worldwide commerce. For example, it allowed shipping companies to plan in advance the best times of the day for their ships to approach and dock at various ports.

By relating the tides to the gravitational pull of the moon and sun, Newton's theory also showed that the length of a day is not fixed and unchangeable. In fact, because of the tides, the day is getting longer. As the tidal bulges make their way around the planet, they rub against the bottoms of the oceans. This very slightly lowers the energy of the Earth's rotation. Having less energy, the Earth must rotate more slowly. Since the length of the day corresponds to the time the planet takes to rotate on its axis, the slower the rotation period, the longer the day.

Of course, the Earth's rotational energy is huge, so it takes a long time for this effect of the tides to be felt. Scientists have calculated that the day is getting longer by about a second every 100,000 years. This does not sound like much until one considers that the Earth is nearly five billion years old.

This means that the day has lengthened by some fifty thousand seconds, or fourteen hours since the Earth came into existence. At that time, the day was only ten hours long!

There is another unexpected twist to this effect of the tidal bulges. As the Earth slows down, the moon is slowly moving farther and farther away. This happens because the energy the Earth loses as it slows down does not just disappear. The Earth transfers that energy to the moon, pushing it away. Eventually, the Earth's rotation will slow to zero, and the same side of the Earth will always face the moon. Then the moon will no longer move away but remain locked in place above the Earth. Also, the moon's tidal bulge will stay in the same place on the Earth, a spot where it will be high tide forever. Luckily, people today need not worry about this chain of events, since it will not come about for many billions of years.

Knowledge of Gravity Advances Civilization

The law of universal gravitation gave people not only the information needed to predict the ebb and flow of the tides; it also gave them a way to predict how the bodies of the solar system would move, from one month or year to the next. This was a great aid to navigation. Navigators made maps of the world with imaginary lines on them. Some lines went up and down, connecting the north and south poles. These were called lines of longitude. Other lines went from side to side. These were called lines of latitude. These sets of lines broke up the map of the Earth's surface into squares.

Sailors could find their locations by checking a map and seeing which square they were in. To calculate the square, they looked at the positions of the heavenly bodies. Thanks to the law

A drawing shows the Earth, moon, and sun as they may look in billions of years. Here, the Earth's rotation has slowed to zero, and the moon remains permanently locked in place. The tides will remain high in the spot directly beneath the moon.

Before the advent of modern navigational aids, sailors analyzed the position of heavenly bodies to determine their location in foreign waters.

of universal gravitation, the height of a heavenly body above the horizon at any time of the year could be predicted. Measuring this height showed the sailors which longitude and latitude they were in. Now commercial ships and fleets of war vessels could plot the exact longitude and latitude of their positions and destinations. This advance, brought about directly by Newton's explanation of gravity, received a further boost in the 1700s. At that time several different chronometers (exact measuring and time-keeping devices) were invented. Significantly, all these advances came at a critical time in history. During the 1700s Europeans were discovering previously unknown, distant lands, and the need for advanced navigational techniques had become essential.

The ability to accurately plot longitude and latitude also aided in the science of cartography, or mapmaking.

For the first time in history, people could accurately determine the sizes and outlines of the various continents, oceans, and seas. This capability helped the European powers to slice up the lands of Africa, Asia, and the Americas into neat parcels for purposes of colonization and exploitation. Thus, scientific techniques developed as a result of the law of universal gravitation indi-rectly affected the destinies of many countries. This illustrates how Newton's ideas on gravity shaped the future of civilization in ways that could not have been foreseen in Newton's own time.

Since Newton, scientists have continued to study gravity and its effects on the Earth. Such studies indicate that the gravitational pull of the planet has affected the course of history in still another way. This effect is less obvious, yet no less significant than advances in navigation and mapmaking.

The Bombardment of the Earth

In the desert near the town of Winslow, Arizona, lies a huge circular depression commonly referred to as Meteor Crater. Nearly a mile across and hundreds of feet deep, the crater has been known for hundreds of years. In the eighteenth and nineteenth centuries, some scientists pointed out that Meteor Crater resembles the craters on the surface of the moon. Most scholars at that time attributed the lunar craters to volcanic activity. Since many craters of volcanic origin can be found in the vicinity of Meteor Crater, it too was thought to be the remnant of an extinct volcano.

Later, astronomers realized that most of the craters on the moon had been caused by impacts with celestial objects. Asteroids, comets, and meteors—hunks of rock and ice from outer space—had periodically been attracted by the moon's gravity and crashed into the moon's surface. The collisions gouged out craters ranging in size from less than an inch across to hundreds of miles in diameter. The Arizona depression was also found to be an impact crater. Later, scientists discovered that the surfaces of Mars, Mercury, and many other celestial bodies are covered with impact craters. Clearly, bodies the size of Mercury and the moon, both less massive than Earth, had undergone many collisions over the history of the solar system. Logically, Earth, having a stronger gravitational pull than either Mercury or the moon, should have sustained more impacts. Why then are there so few impact craters on Earth?

Astronomers point out that Earth has indeed undergone massive bombardment by meteors and other cosmic missiles. However, unlike the moon and most other members of the solar system, Earth has a substantial atmosphere and plenty of liquid water. Over the course of time, the effects of wind,

The Earth undergoes meteor bombardment.

rain, and movements in the planet's crust slowly erode or fill in the craters formed by impacts. Researchers explain that there are two reasons why the Arizona crater has not yet been erased by the elements. First, it is located in the desert, where the effects of erosion are minimal. Second, the crater is a fairly recent formation. Scientists estimate that it originated about twenty-five thousand years ago. At that time, a hunk of rock and metal about seventy-five feet across collided with the Earth. The object approached at a speed of ten to fifteen miles per second, and exploded with the force of a four-megaton nuclear bomb. It probably killed all life within a hundred square miles.

The impact that created Meteor Crater was fatal for any living things that happened to be in the area at the time. But the collision was relatively tiny compared to some of the impact events that have occurred in Earth's more remote past. Researchers have found large circular formations all over the world that are believed to be semieroded impact craters. A few are hundreds of miles across, indicating catastrophes of huge proportions. For instance, evidence suggests that both the Gulf of Mexico and Canada's Hudson's Bay are remnants of gigantic ancient collisions between Earth and objects from space. Impacts like these apparently do not occur very often—

Some scientists believe that a huge comet or asteroid collided with Earth about sixty-five million years ago. They believe the collision was so great that it wiped out the entire dinosaur population.

perhaps only once in several hundred million years or more. But scientists estimate that smaller, still deadly, gravity-induced disasters happen more frequently. These events have the potential to affect the course of Earth's history. Modern studies suggest they have done just that many times.

Nobel prize winner Luis Alvarez and his son Walter are two of many scientists who believe a huge collision event wiped out the dinosaurs about sixty-five million years ago. They are convinced that a comet or an asteroid, perhaps six to ten miles in diameter, struck the Earth. They believe the event caused the extinction of the dinosaurs and many other animal and plant species. Mammals, which were small, rodentlike creatures at the time, were among the survivors of the catastrophe. According to this view, the elimination of large reptilian predators cleared the way for the rise of larger, more advanced mammals. Eventually, say proponents of the theory, this new turn in the course of evolution led to the development of the primates and finally human beings. Similar mass extinctions have occurred throughout the history of life on the planet. The Alvarezes and others think that these events too were caused by giant impacts.

Could a large collision happen today, perhaps destroying an entire city? Apparently just such a disaster almost took place in 1908. During that year a meteor or small comet exploded above a remote region of Siberia in Russia. No people lived in the immediate area. But a man standing more than sixty miles away was knocked off his feet by the pressure wave generated by the blast. Scientists who later investigated the site of the event found entire

Birds soar through the sky, despite gravity's downward pull.

forests completely flattened for hundreds of square miles. Calculations showed that, had the object struck only an hour or two later, a much worse catastrophe would have occurred. By then, the Earth's rotation would have carried the populous Russian city of St. Petersburg (now Leningrad) into the object's path. Millions of people would have been killed. Experts say another large impact might not occur for hundreds or thousands of years. Or such an event might happen next week. There is simply no way to predict such disasters.

The fact that objects, from cannonballs to asteroids, are pulled downward toward the surface of the Earth is not the only thing about gravity that has fascinated people throughout history. Men and women have always marveled at how birds are somehow able to resist gravity's relentless tug. Beginning in ancient times, people imagined what it might be like to be able to jump into the air and keep going. They dreamed of breaking free of gravity and flying.

Knowledge of the workings of gravity made that dream come true.

Breaking Free of Gravity's Bonds

Actual powered flight was not accomplished until the early years of the twentieth century. However, the idea that human beings might fly like birds pervades the ancient myths and legends of many cultures. For example, there is the Greek tale of Daedalus, an architect-inventor who made two sets of artificial wings. He and his son, Icarus, glued on the wings and flew upward to escape from a fortress-prison. Daedalus warned his son not to fly too high because the sun might melt the glue. But Icarus disregarded his father's advice and soared higher and higher. Eventually, as Daedalus had predicted, the glue melted and Icarus fell to his death. The lesson of this and many similar stories seemed to be that humans were not destined to fly.

But some people refused to believe that humans would always be earthbound. They reasoned that God had given human beings intelligence. Using that intelligence, people might find some way to circumvent the ever-present pull of gravity. The Italian artist-engineer Leonardo da Vinci endeavored to find a way when he made drawings of mechanical flying machines. Unfortunately, the technology needed to build motors to power his machines did not exist at the time. Nevertheless, da Vinci's work was important because it inspired later engineers who did possess the necessary technology. For instance, da Vinci's design of a helical screw device led Igor Sikorsky to build the first modern helicopter. And the Italian's drawings of fixed wings, complete with movable flaps, influenced Otto Lilienthal, who designed and flew hang gliders in the 1890s. These gliders, in turn, inspired the work of Wilbur and Orville Wright. On December 17, 1903, at Kitty Hawk, North Carolina, their airplane made

According to Greek legend, Daedalus and Icarus used handcrafted wings to overcome gravity's grip.

the first successful powered flight in history.

But the Wright brothers were not the first human beings to escape from gravity's grip. Unpowered balloons successfully carried human beings thousands of feet into the atmosphere as early as 1783. The early balloons took advantage of the simple fact that heat rises. People filled the balloons with heated air, which lifted the cloth airships off the ground.

Gliders appeared about 1853. Early glider pioneers used the wings of birds as models for the wings of their gliders. The inventors deduced that when birds fly, the air rushes more quickly *over* their wings than *under* them. This creates lower air pressure on the upper part of the wing. The higher air pressure underneath the wing pushes upward, lifting the bird into the air. This process, appropriately called lift, enabled the gliders to defy the pull of gravity. Unfortunately, gliders were very inefficient. They were slow and, like balloons, could travel only where the wind took them.

In the 1890s, Otto Lilienthal prepares to take off in his handcrafted glider.

Before human flight was possible, Leonardo da Vinci made thousands of sketches of mechanical flying machines. His drawings were inspirational to future engineers.

The first dirigible, a large airship filled with hydrogen gas and pushed through the air by a small engine, was launched in 1900. This airship rose upward because hydrogen is lighter than air. The engine allowed the operators to propel the ship in the desired direction at a moderate speed. But dirigibles were dangerous. This fact was graphically demonstrated when the *Hindenburg*, the largest dirigible ever built, exploded and burned in 1937. This disaster, which killed and injured dozens of people, effectively ended the widespread use of such vehicles.

Balloons, gliders, and dirigibles all lifted people off the Earth's surface. This, in a sense, fulfilled humanity's ancient dream of overcoming gravity and flying like the birds. But the future of human flight rested with the motorized airplanes first demonstrated by the Wright brothers. The motors push the planes through the air quickly. The faster a plane moves, the lower the air pressure above the wings and the stronger the lifting action of the air below the wings. Airplanes can fly to great altitudes and achieve speeds of hundreds of miles an hour. Therefore they are very efficient for travel within the Earth's atmosphere.

Even as the Wright brothers and other airplane pioneers labored to perfect their inventions, other visionaries dreamed of taking human flight a step further. Perhaps, they reasoned, the pull of gravity might be overcome completely, allowing people to travel into space. One such visionary was a Russian mathematics teacher named Konstantine Tsiolkovsky. He began publishing serious articles on space travel in 1895, eight years before the Wright brothers made their historic flight! Tsiolkovsky realized that any craft attempting to leave Earth would have to achieve the planet's escape velocity of 7 miles/sec. This speed, he reasoned, could only be attained by the use of rockets.

Rocket propulsion is not a new idea. In fact, rockets have been around for so long that no one knows for sure who invented them. It is generally believed that the Chinese invented the rocket more than a thousand years ago for use in fireworks. They then applied the concept to the battlefield. Rockets using black gunpowder became a regular feature of medieval and even early modern warfare. For example, a mass attack of British rockets destroyed most of the city of Copenhagen, Denmark, in 1807. For centuries, few envisioned that rockets could be used for any other purpose than to kill people.

Tsiolkovsky appears to have been the first person to seriously suggest the use of rockets for travel beyond Earth. He was also the first to realize that gun-

A drawing depicts the Wright brothers during one of their glider experiments. On December 17, 1903, they flew the first powered airplane at Kitty Hawk, North Carolina.

powder was not a powerful enough fuel to achieve the speeds necessary to escape the pull of gravity. He suggested instead a mixture of liquified hydrogen and oxygen. This fuel would burn inside an engine, shooting a stream of exhaust gases from the rear of the rocket. The power of the exhaust would push on the rocket, creating a forward-directed force called thrust. The more powerful the engine, the greater the thrust and the faster the rocket would move. Tsiolkovsky insisted that, if a rocket could reach Earth's escape velocity, it would overcome the pull of gravity and travel into space.

The American rocket pioneer Robert Goddard adopted Tsiolkovsky's idea. He began launching liquid-fuel rockets to great heights in 1926. Goddard dreamed of someday sending a rocket-propelled craft into orbit around the moon. The craft would photograph the far side, which had

HOW AIRPLANES OVERCOME GRAVITY

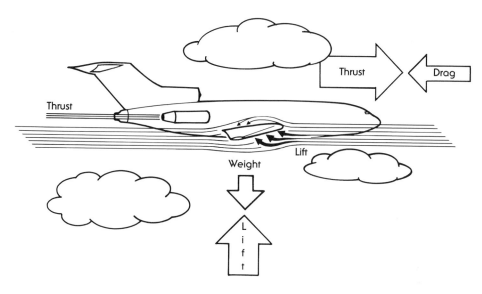

For an airplane to fly, it must overcome two effects of gravity: weight and drag. Weight is the effect of objects being drawn toward the Earth's center of gravity. Drag is the effect of the atmosphere, or air pressure, slowing down moving objects.

An airplane overcomes drag with the thrust from its engines or propellers, and it overcomes weight with lift. The airplane gets its lifting power from the shape of its wings. The wing is flat on the bottom and curved on top. Air passes over the curved top faster than it passes under the flat bottom. This puts more air pressure beneath the wing than above it, so that the wing is pushed up from beneath.

---

never been seen because the same side of the moon always faces Earth.

Later, during World War II, German scientists used Goddard's ideas to build the V-2, a military rocket loaded with deadly explosives. The V-2 killed many people in England until Hitler's Germany was defeated by the Allies in 1945. After the war, scientists in the United States and the Soviet Union made rapid and significant advances in rocketry. In 1957 the Soviets launched the first artificial satellite, *Sputnik I*. Propelled by a liquid- fuel rocket, the satellite managed to attain escape velocity and go into orbit around Earth. This event ignited a "space race" between the United States and the Soviet Union. The race eventually culminated in 1969 with the touchdown of an American spacecraft—*Apollo 11*—on the surface of the moon.

The advent of space travel has been called one of the great events in human history. After being tethered to the Earth by gravity's bonds for thousands of years, humanity at last had the means to leave its ancestral home. It could reach out and explore the uni-

A drawing depicts the German V-2 military rocket. Loaded with explosives, the V-2 killed many people during World War II. (top right)

Robert Goddard poses beside his newly developed rocket. In 1926, he launched the first liquid-fuel rocket. (top left)

The aggressive policies of the German dictator Adolf Hitler spurred advances in American rocket design. (bottom)

verse the ancients held in awe. Using the mathematical tools handed down by such pioneers as Galileo, Kepler, and Newton, modern scientists have taken the human race to its nearest celestial neighbor. But the moon represents merely the threshold of what lies beyond. The solar system beckons. Although people have learned to escape the sway of the Earth, they will eventually have to deal with the gravities of the sun, planets, and other celestial bodies. All of these bodies are separated by unimaginably vast distances. Yet each is held in place by the same force that commands a ball to fall to the ground.

Hurtling Through Space with the Sun

Gravity is the most important force affecting the heavenly bodies. It influences the ways they are formed, how they move in their orbits, and how each affects its neighbors. Held together by their mutual gravitational attractions, Earth and its moon are the most familiar of the heavenly bodies. Because people live on Earth's surface, and because the moon revolves around Earth, the two bodies seem large and important to human beings. Yet Earth and its moon occupy only one small section of a vast system of celestial bodies orbiting the sun. Because the sun is sometimes re-

ferred to by the name Sol, that system, including the sun itself, is called the solar system. The members of the sun's family range in size from microscopic specks of meteoric dust to the giant planets Jupiter and Saturn. Both are many times more massive than Earth. All are held firmly in the grip of the sun's huge gravitational field.

Once launched into space, craft built by humans become, in a sense, new members of the sun's family. They orbit the sun as the planets do. Understanding how gravity works was the key factor in designing and build-

A drawing illustrates how the planets orbit the sun. The planets are held together by the pull of the sun's gravity.

ing these craft. Once people had used airplanes to overcome gravity near the Earth's surface, the next step was to carry the technology of flight into space. People began launching artificial machines into "Earth-space," the immediate vicinity of the Earth and moon, in the late 1950s. These craft utilized the power of rocket thrust to attain speeds in excess of 7 miles/sec. This is the Earth's escape velocity, and attaining this speed allowed the craft to break free of the planet's grip.

Yet, although they had escaped from the Earth, the devices were still bound to the sun's gravitational pull. People on Earth are not physically aware of that pull. It is still, however, the awesome force that dictates the ultimate destination of every body in the solar system. This is because the sun does not stand still. Instead, it moves along at the considerable velocity of 12 miles/sec. As the sun relentlessly hurtles through space, its gravity drags the planets, comets, and any floating spacecraft along with it.

A Civilization in Orbit

The first machines to become new members of the solar system were pilotless satellites launched into Earth orbit. On October 4, 1957, the Soviet Union rocketed *Sputnik I* into orbit. In 1958, the United States also began launching satellites, including early members of the Explorer and Vanguard series. That same year, the U.S. Congress passed the Space Act. This act officially created the National Aeronautics and Space Administration (NASA). NASA coordinates space-related activities for the country.

The early satellites demonstrated that orbiting machines could gather much important information that could not be collected by gravity-bound devices on Earth. For instance, the U.S. Explorer satellites studied interplanetary radiation and magnetic fields. And the Soviets sent *Luna 3* around the moon in 1959. That craft took crude pictures of the moon's far side, fulfilling the dream of American rocket expert Robert Goddard.

Later, more advanced satellites significantly affected business, politics, and everyday life on Earth. Complex weather satellites increased the speed and reliability of forecasts around the world. The improved ability to follow the paths of hurricanes and typhoons alone is estimated to have saved thousands of lives each year since the 1960s. Communications satellites ushered in an age of instant global information exchange. Telephone, radio, and television signals are beamed up to a satellite. They are relayed around the world from one satellite to another, then beamed back down to receivers on Earth. Both international commerce and the entertainment world have greatly benefitted from such advances.

Spy satellites, which gather information about foreign military and industrial capabilities, have profoundly influenced international relations, especially between the United States and Soviet Union. The most notable example occurred in 1962. During that year photographs taken by U.S. satellites identified the presence of Soviet nuclear missile sites in Cuba. Because Cuba lies only a few miles off the coast of Florida, U.S. leaders felt that the missiles posed a threat to the national security. The United States pressured the

Soviets into removing the missiles, but not before the two countries had reached the brink of nuclear war. These events show how knowledge of gravity led to the development of satellite technology. This, in turn, led to tensions between nations.

Pilotless satellites were not the only craft to escape Earth's gravity in the 1960s. The United States and Soviet Union also expended huge sums of money to send human beings into space. Piloted spacecraft, like the pilotless versions, used rocket thrust to achieve escape velocity and overcome the pull of gravity. But piloted craft often have to carry extra life-support items that pilotless craft do not. Such items include food and water, space suits, chairs, communications devices, and special safety equipment. These add weight to the craft, requiring the use of larger, more powerful rockets.

The first person to orbit Earth was Soviet cosmonaut Yuri Gagarin. He made the epic trip on April 12, 1961, in a five-ton capsule called *Vostok 1*. The Soviets also launched the first woman into orbit—Valentina Tereshkova—in 1963. The first American in space was Alan B. Shepard, Jr. Shepard's flight, on May 5, 1961, was the first in the U.S. Mercury program. After Mercury, NASA began the Gemini program, which involved launching two astronauts at a time. Finally came the Apollo program. Each Apollo flight carried three astronauts and prepared the way for the U.S. goal of a moon landing by the end of the 1960s. That goal was achieved on July 20, 1969. On that date *Apollo 11* astronaut Neil Armstrong stepped out onto the powdery soil of the moon and uttered the now famous words, "One small step for a man, a giant leap for mankind."

The moon landing and takeoff were accomplished in the following manner: The *Apollo 11* craft, or capsule, carried a small landing craft named the *Eagle*. Once in orbit around the moon, the *Eagle* separated from the capsule, which remained in orbit. Armstrong pi-

On July 20, 1969, astronaut Edwin Aldrin Jr. walks on the surface of the moon. Aldrin accompanied Neil Armstrong on this historic mission.

The Apollo 11 *lunar module, called the* Eagle, *carries astronauts Neil Armstrong and Edwin Aldrin up from the moon's surface.*

loted the *Eagle* down to the moon's surface. To overcome the moon's gravity and get back up to the capsule, Armstrong fired rockets attached to the *Eagle's* underside. These did not have to be as powerful as the ones that lifted the capsule off Earth because the moon's gravity is considerably weaker than Earth's.

This and later moon landings, though stunning technical achieve-

Astronaut Neil Armstrong smiles from inside the Eagle.

ments, were merely a prelude to a much more ambitious endeavor. This is an on-going process that NASA experts predict will continue into the twenty-first and twenty-second centuries—the industrialization and colonization of Earth-space. This great undertaking will be possible because of the gravity-related discoveries of Newton and other scientists.

The industrialization of space began in the 1970s. The Soviets orbited the first space laboratory, the *Salyut 1* station, in 1971. The seventy-ton American space station, *Skylab,* began operation in 1973. In 1981 the United States introduced the first space shuttle, a large, reusable spacecraft capable of gliding back to Earth and landing like an airplane. The shuttle and its more-advanced offspring will become the space "trucks" that carry raw materials from the Earth and moon into orbit.

Once in orbit, crews of space engineers will use the raw materials to construct huge laboratories. These laboratories will manufacture thousands of

The American space station Skylab *was launched into orbit in 1973, where it remained until 1979. From* Skylab, *scientists gathered data about the sun and Earth. (top)*

A rocket-powered craft defies gravity and shoots toward the moon. (bottom left)

Astronaut Edwin Aldrin conducts experiments during the historic 1969 moon landing. (bottom right)

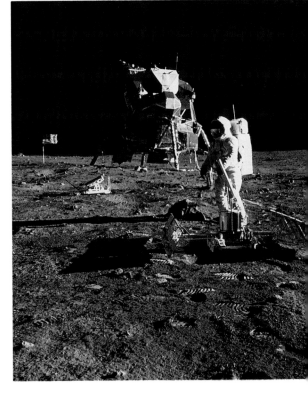

products for later use on Earth. Such items as ball bearings for industry and various lifesaving medicines can be more efficiently produced in the weightless environment of space than under the pull of gravity at the Earth's surface. Earth-space will also support orbiting smelting stations. These will be facilities that use heat to separate metals from rocks. Shuttlecraft will capture meteors and asteroids rich in iron, aluminum, and other useful metals. They will then tow them to the stations. There the metals will be extracted in high-temperature furnaces powered by the free and abundant energy of sunlight. The metals will be used on Earth and also to build more stations in space. The sun will also provide utility stations on Earth with large amounts of energy. Solar-powered satellites will collect the sun's rays and beam their energy via laser beams back to Earth. There the energy will be converted into electricity.

Eventually, say NASA scientists, some space stations will grow into space cities. Tens of thousands of colonists from Earth will inhabit each city. Because the space stations and cities will be permanently inhabited, it will be necessary to provide the workers and colonists with an earthlike gravity. This is because space experiments have suggested that prolonged exposure to weightless conditions may be hazardous to people's health. The production of artificial gravity will be accomplished by spinning the station or city. The spin will produce an outward-moving force called centrifugal force.

A common example of centrifugal force occurs when a person vigorously swings a water-filled bucket in circles. The water is forced outward and held firmly in place in the bucket. The water does not spill out, even when the bucket is turned upside down. Thanks to centrifugal force, people living and working in the outer sections of a spinning space station will experience a pull identical to normal Earth gravity. Because centrifugal force moves outward from the center, the force in the

A drawing depicts the image of a futuristic space city.

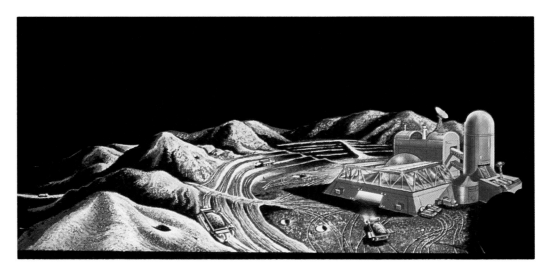

Centrifugal force impels the water in the bucket outward from the source of rotation (in this case, the boy's arm). Thus, the water remains in the bucket and does not succumb to gravity's pull.

center measures zero. So objects located in the center of a spinning station will remain weightless. Consequently, zero-gravity manufacturing areas will be placed in central locations.

Space scientists say the space colonies will also take advantage of another aspect of gravity. In 1772 astronomer Joseph Lagrange demonstrated that five special points exist within the interacting gravity fields of Earth and moon. He calculated that objects orbiting at these spots, now called Lagrangian points after their discoverer, would keep in perfect step with the movements of both bodies. They would also remain "locked" in the same place. Actually, points L1-L3 have since been found to be slightly unstable. This means that objects orbiting in these positions tend to slowly drift away. However, L4 and L5 are extremely stable and will undoubtedly become the sites of many stations and colonies. This is because objects in stable orbital positions make easier targets for spacecraft. Objects that are moving take more time and fuel to approach. Thus flights of personnel and supplies from the moon can be made more simply and cheaply to the L-points than to any other spots in the Earth-moon system.

Eventually, the moon will become more than just a supply base for the civilization in Earth-space. When people are ready to attempt to travel to other planets, launching interplanetary craft from Earth will be difficult and costly. This is because the pull of Earth's gravity is so strong. Since the moon has a weaker gravitational pull, it will be easier and cheaper to launch craft from the lunar surface or from lunar orbit. Thus, the moon will become the jumping-off point for voyages into the depths of the solar system.

A futuristic drawing depicts the moon as a possible supply base for civilizations in space.

The Moon—Departure Point for the Planets

The moon has no life of its own, a fact determined in large degree by the weakness of the moon's gravity. Early astronomers assumed there *was* life on the moon because they thought the moon displayed earthlike conditions. When Galileo trained his telescope on the moon, he saw numerous craters and mountain chains. He also noticed several wide, smooth-looking, darker areas that appeared to be bodies of water. He named these *maria*, the Latin word for seas. Later, Galileo's fellow scientist, Kepler, wrote the first modern science fiction tale, *Somnium*. In this story, Kepler depicted the moon as having not only oceans, but also forests and animal life. Early scientists found it difficult to imagine that God would create another world and not endow it with the benefits of air, water, and life. The concept of a world devoid of life seemed unthinkable.

Yet the moon is just such a dead world. It has no air, no water (except perhaps for some rockbound ice below the surface), and no life of any kind. Scientists believe that the relative weakness of the moon's gravitational pull has been a major cause of this condition. To understand why, first consider the size of the moon. It is 2,160 miles in diameter, about one-fourth the width of Earth. But because it is composed mainly of lighter materials, the moon has a mass only 1/81 that of Earth. Calculations based on the moon's volume and mass indicate a surface gravity about one-sixth that of Earth. This means that if a person who weighs 180 pounds on Earth were to travel to the moon, he or she would weigh only one-sixth as much, or 30 pounds.

Astronomers point out that the moon's gravitational field is not strong enough to hold air and liquid water to its surface. If the body did once possess an atmosphere, it escaped into space long ago. Life as we know it cannot exist without air and water. Therefore, the moon is inhospitable to life (unless such life is protected by space suits, or craft or buildings equipped with their own life-support systems). This suggests that gravity affects the probability of life on celestial bodies. It may be that most objects in the universe the size of the moon or smaller cannot support indigenous (native) life.

Gravity is also responsible for the moon's showing only one side to Earth. The moon's orbital period around Earth is about twenty-nine-and-a-half days. Thus the moon revolves around Earth in approximately one month. At one time, the moon also rotated, or spun on its own axis. This means it had its own day-night cycle. But, say scientists, over the course of millions of years, the pull of Earth's massive gravity slowed down the moon's rotation. This is the same process by which the moon's gravitational pull is presently slowing Earth's rotation. Because the moon is so small, the process for that body was completed more than a billion years ago. The moon has been "locked" with one face toward Earth ever since.

Six Apollo missions visited the moon between 1969 and 1972. The astronauts conducted many experiments that revealed facts about the lunar soil, craters, and composition of the satellite's interior. The most important information concerned the age and formation of the moon.

Gravity played an important part in the formation of the moon, as it does in the formation of all celestial bodies. The exact way this was accomplished has been a topic of controversy for hundreds of years. Modern scientists have variously considered four basic theories. The condensation theory suggests that the moon and Earth originated near each other and at the same time. According to this view, each body formed when hot masses of gas and dust condensed, or became more tightly packed, as gravity pulled the outer layers toward the center. The condensed balls of gas later cooled and hardened becoming Earth and moon.

Another theory, the fission model of lunar formation, suggests that Earth came into being first. Later, because Earth was still soft, it became lopsided. The force of the young planet's rapid rotation then overcame the pull of gravity on the off-center lump. The lump broke away, condensed under the pull of its own gravity, and cooled. It formed the body we know as the moon.

A third theory to explain the origin of the moon is the capture thesis. This idea suggests that the moon formed somewhere else, perhaps as a small separate planet or as a satellite of Jupiter. Some ancient catastrophe then sent the moon flying through the solar system. Eventually, the wandering moon passed near Earth and was captured by the gravitational pull of the larger body.

The most recent and popular idea concerning the formation of the moon is the collision theory. In this version, Earth formed first. For the first few hundred million years of its existence, the planet's gravity pulled in objects of various sizes—debris left over from the formation of the solar system. These objects repeatedly struck Earth. Near the end of this cycle of bombardment, the planet's gravity attracted a large body, which smashed into the still-soft Earth. The force of the impact was so huge that Earth actually fragmented, sending a large chunk of itself into orbit. The colliding body either merged with what was left of Earth or glanced off and escaped into space. The orbiting chunk that was dislodged by the collision then contracted into a sphere by the pull of its own gravity and became the moon.

The lunar collision theory is strongly supported by the evidence gathered during the moon missions. Studies

WAS THE MOON FORMED BY A COLLISION?

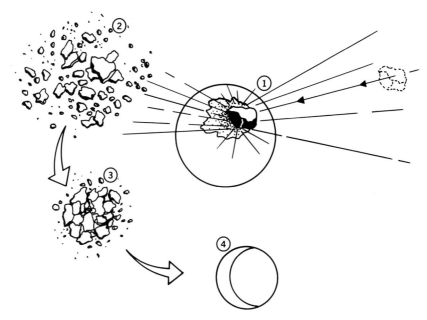

Samples taken from the moon's surface support the theory that the moon was formed just a few million years after the Earth itself, when a large chunk of debris smashed into the still-soft Earth (1). The collision was so great that it sent large fragments of the Earth flying into orbit (2). As they orbited, the gravity of these fragments gradually drew them closer and closer together (3), until they solidified into a single body, the moon (4). Evidence gathered during the Apollo moon missions shows that the moon is composed of the same materials that make up the Earth's outer layers.

found that, unlike Earth, the moon appears to lack an iron core. Instead, the moon is composed almost entirely of lighter materials like those that make up Earth's outer layers. This fits the scenario of the collision theory in which material supposedly splashed from these layers and became the moon.

In addition to learning how gravity shaped the moon, Earth, and other planets, scientists wanted to determine when gravity accomplished this formation process. They reasoned that, by finding the age of the moon, they would also be able to date Earth and even the entire solar system. Reliable estimates of Earth's age are impossible to make on Earth itself. This is because of the effects of billions of years of rain, wind, drifting continents, and volcanic activity. These factors have all but eradicated the original rocks that made up the planet's crust. However, the moon has no rain, wind, or drifting continents, and little, if any, volcanic activity. Thus some of its original rocks are still intact. Studies of the age of these rocks revealed that the moon is about 4.5 billion years old. Presumably, Earth is the same age, since the two bodies are

A drawing shows what life in a space station might be like.

thought to have been formed by gravity at about the same time.

The United States, the Soviet Union, and the European Space Agency are all drawing up plans for building colonies on the moon. When these facilities are built, say space scientists, the moon will take on a new role as a sort of celestial stepping-stone. As mentioned earlier, the moon's low gravity will make it the ideal departure point for bodies in the solar system. Fashioned from the rocks and dust of the lunar soil, huge platforms will take shape at gravity points L4 and L5. These platforms will become the first interplanetary stations. From them, spacecraft will routinely depart for Mars and other bodies held in the grip of the sun.

The Sun—Hub of the Solar System

The force of gravity not only helped shape the moon and Earth, but also governed the formation of the sun and entire solar system. Gravity also influences the process that makes the sun shine. The fact that the sun shines so brightly made it an awe-inspiring object of worship for many ancient peoples. From 1379 to 1362 B.C., the pharaoh Akhenaton ruled Egypt. He was different from all other Egyptian rulers before or since because he pushed aside the traditional gods. He ordained that the face of the sun, or Aton, was the one and true god. Akhenaton's was not the only ancient example of sun worship. Many religions and cults—for instance, Mithraism— looked to the sun as the giver of life. It seemed to make sense. The sun is warm, brings fair weather, causes the crops to grow, and dispels the darkness. But above all, the sun is dazzlingly bright.

The ancients had no way of knowing what actually causes the sun to shine so brightly. Modern science has revealed that the sun is a star, much the same as the few thousand stars visible

by-product. The energy released by trillions and trillions of atoms each second is what forms the sun's huge output of heat and light.

Gravity is the force that provides the heat to start the stellar fusion process. Scientists believe that a star like the sun begins as a huge cloud of gas and dust floating through space. Although it is very thin and spread out, the cloud does have mass. It therefore exerts a gravitational pull. Slowly, under the influence of its own gravity, the cloud begins to contract and becomes more and more compact. The process of contraction produces heat, so the cloud begins to warm up. Driven by the relentless tug of gravity, the process speeds up, and the cloud contracts

Egyptian pharaoh Akhenaton worships the sun. The sun's powerful energy made Akhenaton believe it to be the only true god.

on a clear dark night. Of course, the other stars appear smaller and dimmer because they are so much farther away than the sun. If the sun could be moved to a spot millions of times its present distance, it too would appear as a mere pinpoint of light. Like the other stars, the sun shines because of nuclear reactions that constantly take place in its core. Nuclear fusion is the process that produces the sun's energy. It occurs when two atoms of hydrogen, the lightest element in the universe, are violently driven together, or fused, by intense heat. The result is the formation of an atom of helium, a slightly heavier element, and the release of energy as a

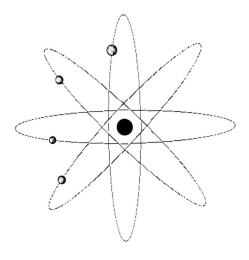

An atom consists of a nucleus and negatively charged electrons. During nuclear fusion, lightweight atoms of hydrogen are driven together to form a heavier element that releases energy.

into a spinning disk that continues to get hotter and hotter. Finally, say scientists, the temperatures at the center of the disk reach the temperature needed to ignite fusion. This produces a sudden burst of brilliant light signaling the birth of a new star. The outer sections of the disk are blown away by an enormous outward rush of heat energy. What remains is a sphere of dense, brightly shining gas like the sun.

As stars go, the sun is rather average. It is some 864,000 miles in diameter and has a volume of more than a million times that of Earth. Temperatures at the sun's surface are about 10,000 degrees, hotter than the hottest furnaces on Earth. Yet this is relatively cool compared with the sun's core, the site of the fusion process. Here, temperatures are estimated to reach 25,000,000 degrees. Because stars are so large, they contain a great deal of hydrogen. Therefore, they can support fusion reactions for a long time. The sun has been shining for several billion years and is expected to continue shining for several billion more.

Because the sun's mighty gravitational pull is what holds the solar system together, scientists have long recognized that the star and its gravity must have played a part in forming the other bodies in the system. Early "catastrophic" theories suggested that a comet or another celestial body crashed into the sun, spewing out material that became the planets. The tidal theory claimed that a passing star came too close and, through its gravitational attraction, drew planetary material out of the sun.

The theory that is generally accepted by scientists today is the nebular hypothesis. This involves the contracting cloud already described in connection with the birth of the sun. Scientists call the original gaseous cloud the primeval solar nebula. According to the nebular hypothesis, as gravity forced

Some scientists believe that a sudden burst of light, such as this one, created the glowing ball of gases called the sun.

The planetary rings of Saturn are bright and conspicuous.

the nebula to contract, lumps formed in the outer sections of the cloud. These lumps, called planetesimals or protoplanets, were pushed away by the wave of heat energy from the igniting star. Later, the planetesimals contracted under the force of their own gravities, just as the solar nebula had done. However, the planetesimals lacked the mass to produce the temperatures needed for fusion. So these smaller objects slowly cooled and became the planets.

One reason that scientists accept the nebular hypothesis is that it seems to explain the observed behavior of the planets. The original solar cloud, including the lumps that later became the planets, was spinning in a certain direction. Therefore, all the planets should still be revolving around the sun in the same direction that the sun is rotating on its axis. And that is exactly what has been observed.

Because the sun is an average star, astronomers believe that this same process of planetary formation is common to most other stars. Support for this idea came in the 1970s and 1980s. At that time, astronomers discovered large disks of gas orbiting several nearby young stars. Presumably these disks are in the process of condensing into plan-etary systems. Thus solar systems may be the rule, not the exception, in the universe.

The Members of the Solar System

The solar system is made up of millions of objects—planets, moons, asteroids, comets, and meteors—all held together by the pull of the sun's gravity. These celestial bodies move through space with their parent star. Nine planets are known to orbit the sun. Moving outward from the star, the first four planets are Mercury, Venus, Earth, and Mars. These are usually referred to as the inner or terrestrial planets. Each is small and rocky. Mercury and Venus have no known satellites; Earth, of course, has one—the moon; and Mars has two tiny satellites—Phobos and Deimos.

Beyond the orbit of Mars, there is an area containing thousands (perhaps millions) of small rocky or metallic objects called asteroids. This area is usually referred to as the asteroid belt. Some scientists say it is possible that the asteroids are the fragments of a former planet that exploded or was pulled apart by the gravitational pull of a

THE SOLAR SYSTEM

larger body. However, most astronomers believe the asteroids are leftovers of the thousands of original planetesimals. These are the lumps that separated from the outer shell of the primeval solar nebula. Meteors—small rocky bodies that resemble asteroids—are not confined to the asteroid belt. They wander randomly through the solar system.

Continuing past the asteroid belt, the next four planets are Jupiter, Saturn, Uranus, and Neptune. These are commonly called the giant planets for obvious reasons. Jupiter, for instance, has a diameter eleven times that of Earth and a volume fourteen hundred times as large! Neptune, the smallest of the four giant planets, is still so large that, if it were hollow, forty-three Earth-sized bodies could fit inside. Though large, the giants are much less com-

The sun and all of the celestial bodies that move around it comprise the solar system.

pact, or dense, than the inner planets. This is because the giants are, like the sun, mainly composed of lighter, gaseous materials. Therefore, although Saturn has a volume 860 times that of Earth, the larger planet is only 95 times as massive.

Because the giant planets have larger gravitational pulls than the inner planets, the giants tend to attract more and sometimes larger satellites. Jupiter has sixteen known moons, the four largest being Ganymede, Callisto, Io, and Europa. These are often called the Galilean moons, after their discoverer, Galileo. Io is particularly interesting because it has many active volcanoes. Each spews sulphur and poisonous gases high above Io's surface. Europa is also unusual. Though it is entirely encased by a shell of ice, scientists theorize that there may be a global ocean of liquid water beneath the frozen surface. Some researchers have suggested that the heat from the satellite's core may have created conditions hospitable to some kind of marine life.

Saturn has seventeen known satellites, the largest being Titan. This satellite is about four-and-a-half times the size of Earth's moon. Studies have indicated that Titan has a dense atmosphere made up of methane gas and oil-like hydrocarbons. Uranus possesses fifteen satellites, and Neptune, eight. Neptune's largest moon, Triton, is slightly larger than Earth's moon and is partially covered by a layer of nitrogen frost.

All four giant planets have ring systems. Saturn's is the largest, brightest, and most beautiful. It appears that gravity plays a part in both the creation and destruction of planetary ring systems. Most scientists think such rings form when one of a planet's satellites gets too close to its parent and is pulled apart by the planet's larger gravity. Although such rings appear solid from a distance, they are actually composed of thousands of small, orbiting chunks of rock and ice. Astronomers believe that planetary rings are not permanent features. In time, a planet's gravity pulls more and more of the ring material down to the surface, and the rings eventually disappear. This means that, because Saturn's rings are so conspicuous, they must have formed comparatively recently.

Far beyond the ringed giants lies the outermost planet, Pluto. Through a telescope, this planet appears as only a pinpoint of light, so it remained undiscovered until 1930. A tiny world, not much bigger than Earth's moon, Pluto is more than thirty-nine times farther from the the sun than Earth is. But even at this great distance, the sun's gravity still manages to hold the remote little world securely in orbit. Pluto takes about 248 Earth-years to make a single revolution around the sun. Because it receives so little of the sun's warmth, Pluto is also the coldest planet. Scientists believe that any atmosphere it might once have possessed is frozen on its surface. Pluto has one moon, Charon.

Despite the fact that it is the farthest planet from the sun, Pluto by no means marks the outer boundary of the solar system. Astronomers believe that, billions of miles beyond Pluto, the sun's gravity holds in place a huge spherical shell of comets. These are mostly tiny (about one to ten miles across) chunks of ice and rock. Scientists think that they number in the trillions and that they are the frozen remnants of the outermost section of the original solar nebula.

Occasionally, gravitational disturbances dislodge a comet and send it slowly spiraling inward toward the sun. After millions of years, it enters the central region of the solar system occupied by the sun and planets. Here, the comet follows Kepler's second law, which dictates that a body speeds up when it approaches the object it orbits. Thus the sun's gravity causes the comet to travel faster as it nears the star. Eventually, the warmth of the sun begins to vaporize the comet's outer layers of ice. This vaporized material becomes the comet's tail. The solar wind, a constant outflowing of tiny particles from the sun's outer atmosphere, forms the tail by pushing the comet's vapor

Workers look skyward as comets stream through the night sky.

Halley's comet streaks through the sky in 1986. It will appear next in 2061.

into space (always in a direction away from the sun).

Drawn by the gravitational pulls of the sun and planets, the comet stays in the inner solar system and repeatedly orbits the sun. If the comet comes close enough to Earth, it becomes visible to the naked eye. The most famous example is Halley's comet, which is visible every seventy-six years.

In its long journey toward the sun, a comet travels across fully one-half the width of the entire solar system. To get an idea of the immense size of the solar system, imagine that the sun is a beach ball 2 feet in diameter. On this scale, Mercury is a tiny pebble orbiting the ball at a distance of about 83 feet. Earth is a slightly larger pebble at a distance of some 214 feet. The moon is a grain of sand 6 inches from the pebble/Earth. Jupiter is represented by a small golf ball located about 1,100 feet, more than one-fifth of a mile, from the beach

ball/sun. Farther away still, more than 1.5 miles from the beach ball/sun, is a grain of sand representing Pluto. Finally, at the outer edges of the model solar system, the comets, represented by microscopic dust particles, orbit at a distance of 2,000 miles!

So far, human beings have managed to traverse only the six inches from pebble/Earth to sand grain/moon. Exploring the farthest reaches of the sun's realm will take generations and require the talents, dedication, and adventurous spirits of millions of people. Yet the solar system is but a tiny fragment of a much larger cosmic structure. Huge as the empty spaces between the planets appear to be, they are small compared with the distances to even the nearest stars. Beyond the solar system loom vast swirling star systems—objects so massive that their gravities completely dwarf the pulling power of the sun.

Measuring the Milky Way

Gravity holds the sun and its entire family of planets, moons, and other bodies tightly in orbit around an object millions of times larger than the solar system. That colossal object, called a galaxy, is a system of billions of stars, all spinning around a common center of gravity. Seemingly countless stars and their planets await exploration by future spacecraft. But, before people can attempt to travel beyond the boundaries of the solar system, they must first break free of the gravity of the sun. To do this, they must find fast and practical ways of traversing the great distances within the solar system itself.

Two factors make such long-distance voyages difficult. First, the speeds so far attained by our spacecraft are too slow. Exploratory craft like the Voyagers, which flew past the four giant planets in the 1970s and 1980s, traveled at velocities of about 20 miles/sec. This seems incredibly fast by Earthly standards. But, these craft would still take six years to reach the planet Pluto. Allowing another six years for the return trip, the voyage to Pluto would require astronauts to be away from home for twelve years. At the same velocity, reaching the cometary shell at the solar system's edge would take about ten thousand years. Journeying to the nearest star (excluding the sun, of course) would take forty thousand years! Clearly, faster speeds must be developed before such trips can become practical.

The other factor that makes long-distance space travel difficult is the energy needed to propel the craft. Voyages lasting years will require large amounts of fuel for accelerating and maneuvering the craft. Much fuel will

The force of gravity holds together this spiral galaxy, composed of gas, dust, stars, and other matter.

Scientists use the slingshot effect when planning outerspace voyages. This effect occurs when the gravitational pull of nearby planets boosts the speed of a spacecraft so that it does not need to use expensive fuel.

also be needed to run the life-support and other onboard systems. One way to help save fuel and energy is to use the force of gravity to help accelerate the spacecraft. This method, called gravity assist, or the slingshot effect, has already been used by NASA scientists in propelling the Voyager spacecraft from one planet to another. For instance, the craft were aimed in such a way that they passed Jupiter at a special angle and distance. The planet's gravity tugged at the craft, boosting their speed and whipping them into a wide curve toward Saturn. Upon reaching Saturn, the craft went through the same procedure and headed for Uranus. Perhaps future interstellar ships will begin their epic journeys by picking up an initial gravity assist from the sun.

The Distances to the Stars

Assuming that the problems of speed and fuel are overcome, the next question for interstellar pioneers to address concerns their destination. Which star should they visit first? Space scientists say it is unlikely that such expeditions, requiring years of planning and huge sums of money, will blindly strike out for a randomly chosen star and hope for the best. Instead, expedition planners will consider many conditions. These will include whether a star has planets, and whether any of these planets might be similar to Earth. Planners will also consider possible indications (such as radio signals) that intelligent creatures already inhabit such planets, and the distances to prospective target stars. Logically, the closest stars that fulfill at least one of the first three conditions will be the best candidates.

Still, even the closest stars are extremely distant. The nearest star to the solar system is Alpha Centauri, which lies at a distance of some 26,000,000,000,000 miles! With so many zeros, this is obviously a large figure. But exactly how large is it? Even astronomers, who constantly work with large figures, do not like the idea of writing all those zeros. They prefer a simpler way of expressing such distances. Replacing the zeros with a word and saying the figure is 26 *trillion* miles certainly helps simplify the situation. A trillion is a million times a million. But there is still a problem. People are used to measuring distances on Earth in hundreds or thousands of miles. Thus, it is difficult, if not impossible, for most people to visualize just how far 26 trillion miles really is.

So astronomers generally use a special unit to express the great distances that lie beyond the solar system. That unit is the *light-year*, which is the distance light travels in a year. Light travels at 186,000 miles/sec, and scientists believe that nothing in nature can travel faster. At this enormous speed, a beam of light could race around the Earth more than seven times in a second. There are 86,400 seconds in a day and 31,536,000 seconds in a year. Multiplying 186,000 miles/sec times 31,536,000 seconds gives the distance light travels in a year—about 6 trillion miles.

Since a light-year is equal to 6 trillion miles, Alpha Centauri, at a distance of 26 trillion miles, is said to be 4.3 light-years from Earth. That means that when people look at Alpha Centauri, the light they are seeing left that star 4.3 years before. Another way of expressing it is: If Alpha Centauri somehow disappeared tonight, people on Earth would not know about it for over four years. During that time, they would still be seeing the light that left the star *before* it disappeared.

Because it is the nearest star, one might expect Alpha Centauri to shine brightly in the night sky, and so it does. It is the third brightest star in the sky. The brightest star, Sirius, also comparatively near, is about 8 light-years distant. But the brightness of a star is not necessarily an indication of its distance.

Canopus, the second-brightest star in the sky, is 650 light-years away. In order to appear so bright at that distance, Canopus must be unusually large and luminous. In fact, it is a supergiant star forty times brighter than the sun. Naturally, such a giant star has a giant gravitational field. This field has the potential to influence a great many objects over a very large distance. Therefore, scientists theorize, Canopus may have a much larger system of planets and moons than the sun has. But space experts point out that visiting any such planets will be extremely time-consuming by human standards. Canopus's distance of 650 light-years is so far that, even if spaceships could travel a thousand times faster than the Voyager spacecraft, a journey to the star would still take over six thousand years!

Such an interstellar trip would appear to be totally impractical. The space travelers would all have died of old age before the journey had barely begun. However, people may someday be able to overcome this problem by building huge, miles-long colony ships. These would be self-contained little worlds. They would include soil to grow crops, libraries with the stored knowledge of humanity, and artificial gravity. Such simulated gravity would be created in the same way it is for space stations—by spinning the ship. The force of the spin would push objects inside the ship away from the center, toward the outer edges. Therefore, the colonists would feel the most Earthlike gravity in the outer regions of the ship.

Those volunteering for a trip in such a craft would be aware that they and their descendants would live out their lives and die on the ship. Finally, after many generations had passed, the

A colony of spaceships explore space.

A drawing shows the three-star system of Alpha Centauri. Gravitational forces lock the stars together so that they appear to be one unit.

craft would reach its destination. Designs for these vessels, called generation ships, are already on the drawing boards. Space scientists point out, however, that it will likely be several decades before people have the technology to build such ships. If and when that day comes, it will be impossible to build the huge craft on Earth or the moon. Such ships would be much too heavy to escape the gravities of these bodies, no matter how large the rockets used. Instead, the builders would assemble the craft in space, where everything, including the craft, would be weightless.

If a generation ship *is* ever built, those on board may choose Alpha Centauri, the nearest star, as their first port of call. Alpha Centauri is actually three stars locked together by their mutual gravitational attractions—a triple star system. Because we humans are 4.3 light-years away, our eyes cannot separate the members of that system, and they appear as one star. Astronomers say human explorers will probably not find many, if any, planets orbiting each star in the Alpha Centauri system. This is because the gravitational fields of the three stars are constantly changing in reference to one another. Because of these complex changes in gravity, say astronomers, the orbit of an Alpha Centaurian planet would probably be unstable. Such an orbiting body would eventually either crash into one of the three stars or fly off into space. However, there is the possibility that some planets might be distantly orbiting the entire Alpha Centauri system. They would treat the combined masses of the three stars as a single center of gravity. Experiencing the spectacular sight of a sky with three suns will, no doubt, be enough of an incentive for the human explorers to stop and visit such a planet.

Perhaps the explorers will decide to single out other multiple star systems. Some of these systems are so distant that it is impossible to visually separate the individual member stars, even through a telescope. But the colonists will have no trouble identifying these systems. They will simply look for the stars that "wobble." Theoretically, scientists explain, a star with no bodies orbiting it should move along through space in a straight line. But if the star has a companion, the companion's gravity pulls on the star. When the companion is on one end of its elliptical orbit, it pulls the star one way. When the companion reaches the opposite end of the orbit, it pulls the star the other way. Thus the star appears to wobble slightly, back and forth, as it moves along. Although the companion (or companions) cannot be seen, it can be detected by its gravitational influence on the other star.

Even if the generation ship explores for tens of thousands of years, it will have time to visit only the stars in the immediate neighborhood of the sun. That neighborhood lies tucked away in one small section of a tremendous, swirling cluster of stars. This object is so massive that its gravitational pull holds billions of worlds tightly within its grip.

The Milky Way Galaxy

For thousands of years, people have observed a faint, cloudlike band that stretches across the night sky. The ancients advanced many different explanations for this girdle of light. The most famous version was that of the Greeks, who suggested the band was milk squirted across the heavens from the breasts of the goddess Hera. This legend inspired the name Milky Way, which has been used ever since.

Galileo solved part of the mystery of the Milky Way when he observed the

This emission nebula is a cloud of gas and dust that absorbs and re-emits the lights of nearby stars.

These irregular galaxies that orbit the Milky Way are known as the Magellanic Clouds.

band through his telescope. He saw that the band is composed of thousands and thousands of very faint stars, whose combined light appears as a cloud to the unaided eye. But Galileo was not able to explain why there are so many stars crowded into one narrow section of the sky. This part of the mystery was solved by later astronomers. They discovered that the band of light seen in the sky is the very distant central section of a single, huge collection of stars, called the Milky Way galaxy. This gigantic body is shaped something like a disk, with pinwheel-like spiral arms that rotate around a central point. The disk is so large that its gravitational field holds some 200 billion stars, along with their respective solar systems, in its grip.

Scientists showed that the sun and every other star visible in the night sky are located in a small section within one of the great spiral's several outer arms. Looking in the direction of the galaxy's center, people see the cloud-like band of the Milky Way. There, the stars are much more densely packed than in the outlying regions where the sun is.

Astronomers estimate that the Milky Way galaxy is about 100,000 light-years in diameter and 2,000–3,000 light-years thick. That means that a beam of light will take 100,000 years to travel from one end of the galaxy to the other. The human generation ship, traveling at the same speed it achieved to reach Canopus (20,000 miles/sec) would take 924,000 years to cross the galaxy.

Visible in the night sky in countries south of Earth's equator are two cloud-like patches visually similar to, but smaller than the band of the Milky Way. These patches were first described by members of Ferdinand Magellan's expedition to the southern hemisphere in the 1500s, so the objects became known as the Magellanic Clouds. Astronomers found that, like the band of the Milky Way, the Magellanic Clouds are also composed of millions of very distant stars. For a long time, no one was able to figure out the distance to the clouds. Scientists assumed they were located inside the Milky Way galaxy itself. However, between 1912 and 1917, two American scientists, Henrietta Leavitt and Harlow Shapley, finally calculated the distance to the clouds. The researchers found that the clouds were located about 180,000 light-years distant, completely outside the disk of the Milky Way.

Astronomers concluded that the Magellanic Clouds are small satellite galaxies of the Milky Way. The three bodies are bound together by their mutual gravitational attractions in much the same way that the three stars of the Alpha Centauri system are bound. The colonists on the generation ship will have to be extremely patient if they decide to visit the Magellanic Clouds. Even at their standard speed of 20,000 miles/sec, a round trip will take them more than three million years.

If human beings ever do make the journey to the Magellanic Clouds, they will do so by escaping the gravitational pull of Earth. In addition, they will escape the pull of the sun, and finally the tug of the entire galaxy. Perhaps the colonists will want to linger a few thousand generations and explore the star systems of the Milky Way and its satellites. Eventually, curiosity and the spirit of adventure might compel a few hardy pioneers to strike out across the vast gulfs of intergalactic space. There they will find that the force of gravity does not diminish. Instead, it rules the motions of structures tens of millions of light-years across, with thousands of times the mass of the Milky Way.

Galaxies Beyond Counting

In the 1770s, while searching for comets, the French astronomer Charles Messier noticed several small fuzzy objects in the night sky. Unlike comets, which move across the heavens, Messier's objects remained fixed in place year after year. He called them nebulae, Latin for fogs or mists. Messier compiled a catalogue of nebulae, and these objects are still referred to as M1, M2, and so on, in honor of Messier. By the 1850s, larger telescopes revealed that many of Messier's nebulae had spiral shapes. Astronomers argued about the distances and natures of these objects. Some thought the spi-

This cloud of gas and dust is located in the Sagittarius constellation.

rals were swirling gas clouds located within the Milky Way. Others insisted that the nebulae were distant galaxies, or island universes, similar in size to the Milky Way itself.

Finally, in 1924, American astronomer Edwin Hubble proved that the spiral nebulae were indeed galaxies in their own right. He and other astronomers calculated the distances to these galaxies. The nearest is a large spiral that appears to the naked eye as an oval-shaped hazy patch in the constellation (star group) of Andromeda. This galaxy is variously referred to as the Great Nebula in Andromeda, the Andromeda galaxy, or M31 (as it appears in Messier's catalogue). Located

Scientists can detect galaxies millions of light-years away with radio telescopes like this one.

at a distance of about 2 million light-years, the Andromeda galaxy is the most distant object visible to the naked eye. The galaxy is so far away that, even when viewed through the largest telescopes, its individual stars cannot be made out by the eye alone. Astronomers must make photographic exposures of several hours in order to gather enough light to make these stars stand out individually. Scientists believe the Andromeda galaxy is similar to the Milky Way in size, shape, and number of stars.

Astronomers found that galaxies can be seen in every direction (except toward the center of the Milky Way, which obscures the view). Some lie only slightly farther away than the Andromeda galaxy. Others are tens, even hundreds, of millions of light-years away. In fact, galaxies continue to extend outward to the very limit of the powers of optical (light-gathering) telescopes. Astronomers refer to that limit as the edge of the visible universe; however, they know the universe does not end there. Scientists use radio telescopes—large devices that gather radio waves instead of light—to study objects that lie beyond the range of optical telescopes. Even at the limits of the largest radio telescopes, more than 2 billion light-years, galaxies have been detected. Astronomers estimate that there are at least several billion galaxies in the universe.

After careful studies of the distribution and directions of motion of thousands of galaxies, scientists concluded that these island universes are attracted to each other by gravity. The pull of gravity appears to cause the galaxies to be unevenly distributed throughout space. Also, most galaxies belong to

THE BIG BANG THEORY

1. All the matter in the universe was once part of a single, hot, dense object called the *primordial egg,* this object exploded, sending hot gases and debris outward in all directions.

2. Gradually, the gravity of the larger masses attracted smaller masses to them, forming stars and planets.

3. As the stars continue to hurtle through space, some planets are moving at just the right speed to be drawn into orbits around them. Just as planets are captured in orbit around stars, smaller bodies, or moons, are captured in orbit around the planets. Similarly, entire solar systems are captured in orbits around galaxies, like the Milky Way. And entire galaxies revolve around still larger galaxies.

huge clusters. Due to gravitational attractions, the individual members of a cluster move through space together, as if they were part of one colossal object. The number of galaxies in a cluster varies. For instance, the Milky Way, Magellanic Clouds, Andromeda galaxy, and about two dozen other galaxies make up a cluster known as the Local Group. By comparison, the more distant Virgo cluster contains several thousand galaxies, and some clusters are made up of tens of thousands of galaxies. These are the largest known structures in the universe.

No one knows the exact size of the universe, but astronomers have made educated guesses about its age. They believe that all the matter in the universe was once part of a single, very hot

and dense object called the cosmic or primordial "egg". For reasons unknown, the egg exploded, and its matter shot outward in every direction. Later the hot matter cooled and condensed into galaxies of stars and planets. This explanation for the beginning of the universe is called the big bang theory. Scientists reason that, if the big bang actually occurred, the galaxies should still be moving outward in all directions. Observations confirm that this is exactly what is happening. Astronomers try to imagine the galaxies moving backwards to their original starting point. The scientists attempt to measure how fast these objects are moving. If they know the speed, they can estimate how long it took for the galaxies to get from the starting point to their

The theories of physicist Albert Einstein profoundly influenced twentieth-century scientific thought.

voyages to other galaxies would last thousands of times longer still. Space experts doubt that people will find such seemingly endless journeys either practical or desirable. Unfortunately, simply increasing the speed of the ship is not necessarily the answer to the problem. Suppose that the ship could be modified to travel at a hundred times the speed of light. A round trip to Andromeda, the nearest galaxy, would still take forty thousand years. Such speeds are purely fanciful anyway, for there is a limit to how fast things can travel.

The Cosmic Speed Limit

In 1905, the German physicist Albert Einstein (1879–1955) announced his special theory of relativity. One of the provisions of the theory holds that the speed of light is the highest possible velocity attainable. Ever since Einstein proposed his theory, scientists have tested it using both mathematics and direct experimentation. So far, the theory has withstood every test, and scientists generally accept its validity.

After setting the speed limit for prospective space travelers, Einstein went on to define the structure of space itself. In 1916 he proposed his general theory of relativity, in which he offered a completely new way of looking at gravity. This idea sparked a scientific revolution the like of which had not been seen since the days of Newton.

present positions. This is the amount of time since the big bang, or the age of the universe. Estimates by astronomers for the age of the universe range from ten to twenty billion years.

Will human beings ever be able to visit remote sections of the universe? Most scientists do not think so. Even the hypothetical trips made by the generation ship across the Milky Way and to the Magellanic Clouds would consume hundreds of thousands, perhaps millions of human generations. And

■■■■■■■■■ CHAPTER **6**

Coping with the Curvature of Space

In his general theory of relativity, Einstein discussed the concepts of mass and gravity. Using only mathematics and logical deduction, he made many predictions about the nature and movements of the celestial bodies. His theory profoundly affected every discipline of physical science because it offered an explanation for gravity very different from the one proposed by Newton. Newton conceived gravity as a force belonging to and exerted by material objects. In Newton's view, the more massive the object, the larger the gravitational force it exerts. Einstein argued that gravity is *not* a force, but instead, a property of space itself.

Einstein's Curved Space

Before Einstein, scientists assumed that space was an empty void with no ability to affect the material objects that moved within it. Einstein envisioned space as having certain properties of its own. These include an invisible "fabric" with a bendable, or elastic, quality. When an object having mass moves through space, Einstein explained, it sinks into the elastic fabric of space and forms a depression. The more massive the object, the deeper the depression it forms. Thus massive objects distort or curve the fabric of space. This curvature is what people experience as gravity.

Einstein argued that when two objects of differing size approach each

Albert Einstein demonstrates one of his many mathematical theories. According to Einstein's theory of relativity, gravity is a property of space itself.

other, the smaller object begins to follow the curve in space formed by the larger object. The smaller object then rolls "downhill" toward the larger object. If the smaller object is moving fast enough, it is able to roll back out of the curve and continue on its way. If, on the other hand, it is moving too slowly, it cannot gain the momentum to escape the depression in space formed by the larger object. The smaller object is then trapped and either orbits around or smashes into the larger object.

GRAVITY: CURVED SPACE

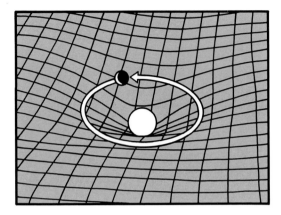

According to Einstein's general theory of relativity, gravity is not a force exerted by material objects but a property of space itself. We can picture space, according to this theory, as an infinite elastic net. Every object in the universe that has mass sinks into this net and makes a depression. The greater the mass of an object, the deeper the depression it makes. These depressions are what we experience as gravity. Einstein called them gravity wells.

When two objects in space approach each other, the lighter of the two rolls into the gravity well of the other. The lighter object will also distort the gravity well of the heavier object to some degree. However, if it is moving fast enough, the lighter object will roll out of the larger object's gravity well and continue moving through space. If it is traveling at exactly the right speed (the escape velocity), it will continue to circle around and around in the gravity well. This is what we observe as an orbit. If the lighter object is moving too slowly to escape the gravity well or to stay in orbit, it will fall into the larger object.

To illustrate this situation, scientists use the example of a thin sheet of rubber stretched tightly in a horizontal position. This represents the fabric of space. The two objects are represented by metal balls. The balls sink into the rubber, forming depressions, or gravity wells. The gravity well formed by the heavier ball is wider and deeper than the other. When the lighter ball gets too close to the heavier ball's well, the lighter ball begins to spiral downward toward the heavier ball. If the sheet of rubber now becomes invisible, the heavier ball appears to be "pulling in" the lighter ball. Thus the heavier ball gives the false impression that it is exerting a force on the other ball.

The test for Einstein's new theory of gravity centered around how his hypothetical gravity wells would affect a beam of light. If space is filled with invisible curves, as Einstein suggested, those curves should bend, or deflect, the path of the beam. If, on the other hand, gravity is a force directly exerted by objects with mass, there should be no deflection because light has no mass. Light should then travel only in a straight line. Einstein insisted that light does bend and that no one had observed this because light travels so fast. He argued that the deflection of light by the gravity wells of normal-sized objects is so small that even the most delicate instruments cannot detect it. Only when light passes by a tremendously massive body, said Einstein, is the bending of light by curved space at all noticeable. Since the sun is the most massive object in the solar system, it seemed the logical choice of a body to test the theory. So Einstein predicted how the sun would deflect the light from a distant star.

The only time the stars can be seen near the sun is during a total solar eclipse, when the moon temporarily blocks the sun's image. Scientists decided to test Einstein's theory during an eclipse that occurred in 1919. The scientists found that the starlight was deflected by nearly the exact amount predicted by Einstein. Confirmation of

the theory of relativity immediately changed the way scientists viewed gravity and made Einstein an international celebrity.

Einstein did not disprove Newton's theory of gravitation. Newton's formulas are still valid in that they can be used to measure gravitational attractions and predict the motions of the celestial bodies. Einstein built upon Newton's work by demonstrating that the underlying cause of those attractions and motions is different than had been supposed. Gravity, said Einstein, is not a force emanating from a body, but the effect of curved space on that body. However, since gravity "behaves" like a force, scientists still use the term force when referring to gravity. And they still explain gravitational effects in terms of Newton's force as well as Einstein's curved space.

Einstein's theory also suggested that objects with unusually deep gravity wells might exist. Theoretically, these objects would bend light so powerfully

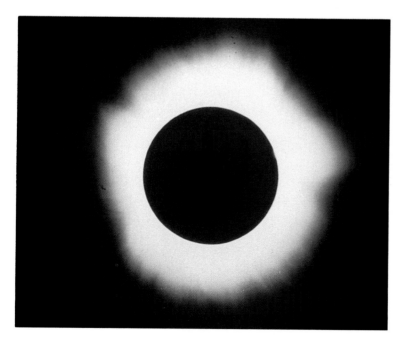

A total eclipse, such as this, occurs when one celestial body completely obscures another.

A red giant star contains an extremely hot core and comparatively cool outer layers. When the red giant burns up all of its fuel, it ends its life as a white dwarf.

that the energy of that light would be lowered. In 1925, scientists confirmed the existence of objects that affected light exactly as Einstein had predicted. These strange, small, yet very massive objects are known as white dwarfs. Later, scientists detected the existence of objects much smaller than white dwarfs, yet many times more massive. Called neutron stars and black holes, these objects possess the most intense gravitational fields in the universe. Not only did Einstein's gravity theory indicate the existence of these objects, it also explained how their immense gravities worked. However, it did not explain how such supermassive objects formed. Scientists looked for the answer to this riddle in the catastrophic death throes of stars.

The Power of Collapsing Stars

Just as human beings are born, live out their lives, and finally die, stars too undergo a life cycle. Scientists believe that a star's cycle begins as outlined in the nebular hypothesis: A huge cloud of gas and dust contracts until it gets hot enough to ignite nuclear fusion. The fusion process converts the star's hydrogen into helium, giving off heat and light in the process.

Scientists have calculated that the extreme heat generated in the center of a star constantly radiates outward, creating pressure. At the same time, the star's massive outer layers tend to roll down into the star's own gravity well. They would keep on rolling if not for the outward-moving heat pressure. When the heat pressure exactly counteracts the inward-moving effect of gravity, the star is said to be stable. As long as it continues to burn hydrogen at approximately the same rate, an average star will shine for ten billion years or more.

Astronomers say that eventually, near the end of its life, a star reaches a point where it has used up almost all of its hydrogen fuel. The core of the star gets hotter and begins to fuse helium and even heavier elements. The additional heat output upsets the balance between heat pressure and gravity, and the outer layers of the star begin to swell. As its core continues to heat up, the star changes color and expands into a red giant, a vast sphere millions of miles across. Scientists predict that the sun will become such a red giant in perhaps five billion years. They estimate that, at maximum expansion, the sun's outer layers will extend to the orbit of Venus (sixty-seven million miles) or more. This will mean the end of life on Earth, for the planet will be reduced to a charred cinder.

Scientists estimate that a star remains a red giant for only a few million years, a tiny fraction of its entire life cycle. Finally the star uses up all of its fuel, and there follows what is perhaps the greatest catastrophe in all of nature—stellar collapse. As the fusion reactions in the star's core cease, the core no longer generates the enormous heat pressure needed to counteract the pull of the star's own gravity. In a matter of mere minutes, say astronomers, the outer layers collapse into the star's gravity well. The collapsing material rolls down and crashes into the star's core in the bottom of the well. The huge force of the collapse compresses the material of the star into a small, yet extremely dense ball—a white dwarf. The compression of so much material into so small a space makes the gravity well even deeper than it was before.

An average white dwarf is only about the size of Earth, tiny considering that most of the mass of the original star is still present. In fact, the matter in a white dwarf is so compact that a small amount of it is extremely heavy. According to astronomers, a piece of white dwarf material the size of a matchbox weighs a thousand tons. The pull of a white dwarf's gravity is huge. An object attempting to leave the surface of such a body would have to attain an escape velocity of more than 3,000 miles/sec, a thousand times that of a normal star.

Once a star becomes a white dwarf, it slowly cools. Eventually all of its heat

A white dwarf is a small yet extremely dense star.

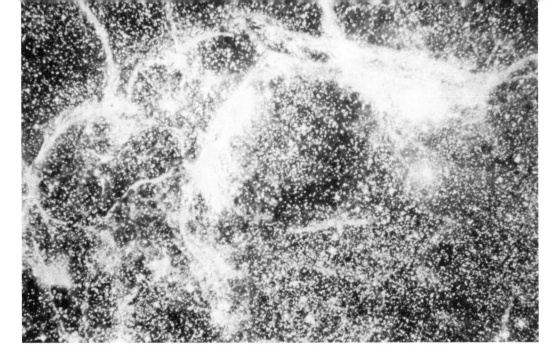

A supernova occurs when an extremely large star explodes after reaching a maximum brightness.

is lost, and it drifts through space as a black dwarf, a burned-out hunk of cosmic debris. This, scientists say, is the fate of average-sized stars like the sun.

But not all stars are the size of the sun. Many are several times more massive. Because they have more mass and thus more powerful gravities, their death throes initiate a chain of events even more violent than those leading to the formation of white dwarfs. Astronomers explain that when a star having a mass three to five times that of the sun runs out of fuel and collapses, two things happen. First, as the collapsing layers of the star approach the core at the bottom of the gravity well, the vast energy exerted by the collapse suddenly converts into heat. Within seconds, temperatures of billions of degrees are

Scientists believe neutron stars form when matter is so dense that the protons and electrons pack together to form neutrons.

A black hole is a hypothetical region in space thought to be caused by the collapse of a huge star.

generated, causing the star to explode. For a few days or weeks, the star shines with the brilliance of millions of suns. Scientists call such an exploding star a supernova.

A supernova explosion hurls a great deal of material into space. However, much of the star's original material remains in the core, where the awesome collapse continues. Here, the gravity well is so deep and narrow that the atoms become distorted. Usually, atoms contain three kinds of particles—protons, neutrons, and electrons. But in the distorted atoms, the protons and electrons combine to form more neutrons. So the result of the collapse is a superdense ball made up almost entirely of neutrons—a neutron star.

Scientists estimate that a neutron star is only about ten to twelve miles across. The star is so dense that a matchbox full of its material would weigh at least a trillion tons. And a neutron star's gravity is so powerful that it makes a white dwarf's gravity seem feeble by comparison. In order to escape from a neutron star's extremely deep gravity well, a body would have to attain an escape velocity of nearly 125,000 miles/sec, about two-thirds the speed of light.

A neutron star is the final stage in the life of a star having a few times the mass of the sun. But what about stars that are larger still? Some stars have as much as fifty to seventy times the sun's mass or more. When such a star collapses, gravity reaches its ultimate power. The fabric of space is greatly distorted, creating what is perhaps the strangest thing in the universe—an object with a bottomless gravity well.

Black Holes—Monsters of the Universe

Einstein's theory of gravity proposed that objects with mass form wells in the fabric of space. The more massive the object, said Einstein, the deeper the well. And it follows that it is more difficult for an object to escape from a deep well than from a shallow one. Therefore, deeper wells have higher escape velocities. Einstein and the scientists of his day considered what might happen if an object had a gravity well so deep that its escape velocity exceeded the speed of light. Since even light could not escape from the well of such a supermassive object, the object could not be seen. (It is because all objects reflect light that they can be seen.) The object would be a black hole in the fabric of space. The scientists concluded that, since nothing can travel faster than light, anything that entered a black hole, including light, could never come out. Therefore, the gravity well of a black hole would be a bottomless pit. One way to visualize this is to imagine that the object is so massive and dense that it never stops falling down its gravity well. The well gets deeper and narrower forever. Therefore, anything that rolls into the well, including light, also plummets downward forever.

Although Einstein's relativity theory showed mathematically that black holes *might* exist, astronomers had no direct evidence for black holes until the 1960s. At that time, satellites picked up strong

bursts of X rays coming from outer space. Scientists had detected X rays from space before. Every star, including the sun, emits X rays along with visible light and other types of radiation. But the new X ray sources were not stars. In fact, astronomers could find no visual objects at all at the locations of the sources. The scientists suspected that such sources might be black holes. They explained how a black hole would emit X rays in the following manner: The X rays do not come from the black hole itself, since nothing can escape from the gravity well of the hole. As the hole moves through space it encounters interstellar gases and debris, which spiral into the well. Just before passing the point of no return at the edge of the well, the debris' atoms are violently torn apart by the hole's immense gravity. As the atoms are annihilated, they emit a burst of X rays, which is eventually detected on Earth.

In 1965, astronomers found an unusually powerful X ray source near a faint star in the constellation of Cygnus. The X rays appeared to come from an

The gravity well of this hypothetical black hole is so great that even light cannot escape its pull.

A BLACK HOLE

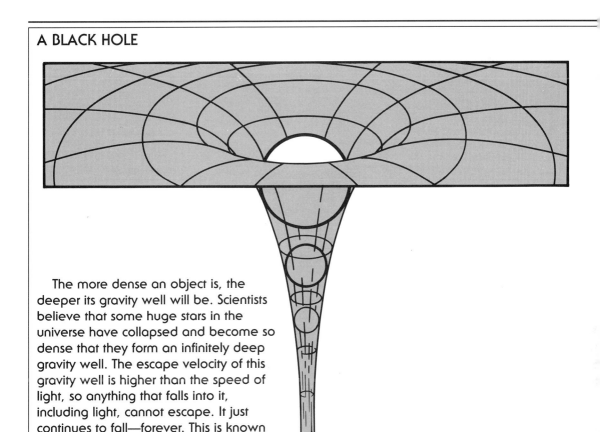

The more dense an object is, the deeper its gravity well will be. Scientists believe that some huge stars in the universe have collapsed and become so dense that they form an infinitely deep gravity well. The escape velocity of this gravity well is higher than the speed of light, so anything that falls into it, including light, cannot escape. It just continues to fall—forever. This is known as a black hole.

invisible object orbiting the star. Scientists named the object Cygnus X-1. Using Newton's formulas, they calculated that Cygnus X-1 has a mass five to eight times that of the sun. This is too large for either a white dwarf or neutron star. Therefore, most astronomers believe that Cygnus X-1 is a black hole. They say that the hole seems to be slowly stripping away the outer layers of the nearby star, and that eventually the entire star will be consumed. The scientists say that the doomed star and Cygnus X-1 used to be companions in a double star system. Thus Cygnus X-1, a black hole, was once a star.

Astronomers explain that a star becomes a black hole by the same process that forms white dwarfs and neutron stars—stellar collapse. When the mass of the original star is large enough, the crushing force of the final gravitational collapse does not stop at either the white dwarf or neutron star stage. Instead, the huge rush of matter down the gravity well continues until the atoms that make up the star's core are ripped apart and their remnants squashed tightly together. The result is a small, massive object inside a gravity well so deep that even light cannot escape it—a black hole.

A black hole, say scientists, can be any size. For example, a black hole with the mass of Earth would be about the size of a golf ball. With a mass equal to

Scientists believe that interstellar gas is sucked into the massive gravitational wells of black holes.

that of the sun, a black hole would be as large as an automobile. Scientists estimate that Cygnus X-1, with a mass five to eight times that of the sun, is the size of a small house. Since Cygnus X-1 is sucking in the material of its companion star, the black hole is getting larger. If it later consumes other nearby stars, it will grow still larger. Astronomers suggest that such a black hole might continue to absorb stars, planets, and any other material it encounters.

Some black holes may grow extremely large. Scientists have detected gigantic X ray sources at the centers of many galaxies, including the sun's own Milky Way. One theory proposes that these sources are supermassive black holes, each containing the material of billions of stars. Called "monstrous cosmic-eating-machines" by one astronomer, such black holes may use their huge gravities to draw in and consume all the matter in their parent galaxies.

Could all the matter in the universe eventually become part of one supergiant black hole? Some scientists think so. In fact, they suggest that the formation of such an object might be part of a recurring universal cycle: The cosmic egg explodes. Hot matter rushes outward, cools, and condenses into galaxies of stars. Some stars live out their lives, then collapse, forming black holes. A few black holes form near galactic centers, where the stars are numerous and tightly packed. These black holes grow huge and absorb whole galaxies, and then clusters of galaxies. Finally, the gravitational attractions of the black holes draw them together. They contract into one superdense object—the next cosmic egg. The egg becomes unstable, explodes, and a new universe is formed. It too eventually collapses under the pull of its own gravity, and the grand cycle is repeated again and again. More cautious astronomers disagree with this dramatic scenario. They say there is not enough matter in the galaxies to create the gravity required for such a cosmic collapse. They suggest instead that the universe may continue to expand forever.

Scientists may argue about the fate of the universe, but they all agree about the role of gravity in nature. By pulling things toward a common center, gravity creates order out of chaos, as when a formless cloud of gas and dust became the sun and planets. And gravity is everywhere. Whether viewed as a force or as a curve in the fabric of space, gravity is part of the underlying structure of things both large and small. As Newton deduced from the fall of an apple, the invisible power that so gently guides a leaf to the ground also propels the largest bodies in the farthest reaches of the heavens.

Glossary

accelerate: To move faster and faster.

asteroid: A chunk of rock and metal orbiting the sun.

asteroid belt: The area between Mars and Jupiter where most of the asteroids orbit the sun.

astrology: A pseudoscience that promotes the belief that the heavenly bodies directly influence the lives of human beings.

astronomy: The science that is concerned with the natures and motions of the celetial bodies.

atom: A tiny building block of matter.

big bang theory: The concept that holds that all the matter in the universe was once part of a single, very dense object; the object exploded, giving rise to the galaxies, stars, and planets.

billion: A thousand times a million.

black dwarf: The burned-out remains of a white dwarf star.

black hole: A superdense object formed from the collapse of a very large star; a black hole's gravity is so strong that even light cannot escape from it.

cartography: The art or trade of mapmaking.

chronometer: An extremely accurate time-keeping device.

comet: A small chunk of ice and rock orbiting the sun; when a comet nears the sun, some of the ice vaporizes and forms a tail.

cometary shell: A huge sphere of orbiting comets that surrounds the sun at a distance of several trillion miles.

constellations: Groups of stars in the night sky to which people have assigned the shapes and names of persons, animals, or objects.

cosmic: Having to do with the cosmos.

cosmic egg: In the big bang theory, the original dense object that exploded to become the known universe.

cosmos: The universe; everything that lies beyond Earth.

decelerate: To move slower and slower.

dirigible: A large airship filled with hydrogen or helium gas and propelled through the air by a small motor.

earth-space: The immediate area surrounding Earth and moon.

ellipse: A closed curve shaped like an oval; Johannes Kepler found that the planets and other celestial bodies move in elliptical orbits.

escape velocity: The speed an object must attain to escape from the gravitational pull of a large body.

fabric of space: A property of space described by Albert Einstein; the fabric bends under the influence of a body with mass, creating a curve or depression.

galactic cluster: A group of galaxies bound together by their mutual gravitational attractions.

galaxy: A large swirling disk of stars; for instance, the Milky Way galaxy, which contains the solar system.

generation ship: A proposed spacecraft large enough to support a population of hundreds or thousands of people indefinitely.

geocentric universe: A universe in which the Earth is the center.

gravitational constant: A mathematical value derived by Isaac Newton for his gravity formula; written as G, its value remains the same regardless of the other factors in the formula.

gravity: The force of attraction exerted between two or more bodies.

gravity assist: Also called the slingshot effect, a method by which a spacecraft uses the gravitational pull of a planet or other large body to propel itself in a prearranged direction.

gravity well: As proposed by Einstein, a depression in the fabric of space caused by an object having mass.

heliocentric universe: A universe in which the sun is the center.

helium: The second-lightest element in nature.

hydrogen: The lightest and most abundant element in nature.

inertia: The tendency of a body to remain either at rest or in motion unless disturbed by an outside force.

intergalactic: Between galaxies.

interplanetary: Between planets.

interstellar: Between stars.

light-year: The distance light travels in one year.

maria: (From the Latin for "seas") broad, flat areas on the moon.

mass: The amount of matter contained in a body.

meteor: A hunk of rock and/or metal that wanders through space.

Milky Way: A narrow, cloudlike band of light faintly visible in the night sky; this band of light is actually the central region of the Milky Way galaxy, which contains our solar system.

million: A thousand times a thousand.

nebula: (From the Latin for "fog") a small cloudy patch in the night sky which may actually be a cluster of stars, a cloud of gas lit up by nearby stars, or a distant galaxy; plural is nebulae.

nebular hypothesis: The concept that holds that the sun and other stars condensed out of large swirling clouds of gas and dust.

neutron star: An unusually dense object formed from the collapse of a star with a few times the mass of the sun; the star is composed almost entirely of neutrons—tiny particles with no electric charge.

nuclear fusion: The process that makes the stars shine; under the influence of great heat, atoms of hydrogen are fused together to form atoms of helium, releasing energy as a by-product.

orbit: The path one celestial body takes in revolving around another.

planet: A body formed from and orbiting around a star.

planetary period: The amount of time a planet takes to revolve around its parent star; a planet's year.

planetesimal: A small, semisolid object that has condensed from a stellar gas cloud and that will combine with others of its kind to form a planet.

protoplanet: A large planetesimal; a planet-in-the-making.

red giant: The last stage in the life cycle of a star; increased heat from the star's core causes the star to swell and change color.

revolve: To orbit around a central point, as when the Earth revolves around the sun.

rotate: To spin on an axis, as when the Earth rotates once in a day.

satellite: A body that revolves around a planet; can be natural, like the moon, or artificial, like a weather device.

Sol: A proper name for the sun.

solar eclipse: An event in which the moon passes between the Earth and the sun, temporarily covering the image of the sun.

solar system: The planets, satellites, comets, and other bodies that are held in place by the gravitational pull of the sun; or such a system around another star.

solar wind: A stream of tiny, energetic particles emitted from the sun's outer atmosphere.

star: A large ball of hot gas; it shines as a result of nuclear fusion reactions in its core.

stellar: Having to do with stars.

stellar collapse: The final stage in the life cycle of a star; the nuclear reactions cease, and the star's material crashes inward under the pull of its own gravity.

supernova: A huge stellar explosion that immediately precedes the collapse of a star.

technology: The application of science and its discoveries to commerce, industry, and everyday life.

trillion: A thousand times a billion.

universe: The sum total of everything that exists.

white dwarf: A very dense object that forms from the collapse of a sunlike star; an average white dwarf is about the size of the earth.

X-ray source: A spot in the sky from which X rays are emitted; some such sources are thought to be black holes.

For Further Reading

Isaac Asimov, *From Earth to Heaven*. New York: Avon Books, 1964.

Isaac Asimov, *Jupiter, the Largest Planet*. New York: Ace Books, 1975.

Isaac Asimov, *The Solar System and Back*. New York: Avon Books, 1959.

William K. Hartmann, et al., *Cycles of Fire, Stars, Galaxies and the Wonders of Deep Space*. New York: Workman Publishing, 1984.

William K. Hartmann, et al., *Out of the Cradle, Exploring the Frontiers Beyond Earth*. New York: Workman Publishing, 1987.

Robert S. Richardson, *The Fascinating World of Astronomy*. New York: McGraw-Hill, 1960.

Carl Sagan, *Cosmos*. New York: Random House, 1980.

Joseph Schwartz and Michael McGuinness, *Einstein for Beginners*. New York: Pantheon Books, 1979.

Works Consulted

Isaac Asimov, *Asimov on Physics*. New York: Avon Books, 1976.

Isaac Asimov, *Beginnings*. New York: Berkley Books, 1987.

Isaac Asimov, *The Collapsing Universe*. New York: Simon and Schuster, 1977.

Isaac Asimov, *Fact and Fancy*. New York: Avon Books, 1962.

Lincoln Barnett, *The Universe and Dr. Einstein*. New York: Mentor Books, 1948.

Hubert J. Bernard, et al., *New Handbook of the Heavens*. New York: Mentor Books, 1959.

Stephen W. Hawking, *A Brief History of Time*. Toronto/New York: Bantam Books, 1988.

James E. Oberg and Alcestis R. Oberg, *Pioneering Space*. New York: McGraw-Hill, 1986.

Gerard K. O'Neill, *2081, A Hopeful View of the Human Future*. New York: Simon and Schuster, 1981.

Jay M. Pasachoff, *Astronomy: From the Earth to the Universe*. Philadelphia: W.B. Saunders Co., 1979.

Bertrand Russell, *The ABC of Relativity*. New York: Mentor Books, 1958.

Index

About the Author

Don Nardo is an actor, makeup artist, film director, composer, and teacher, as well as a writer. As an actor, he has appeared in more than fifty stage productions, including several Shakespeare plays. He has also worked before or behind the camera in twenty films. Several of his musical compositions, including a young person's version of H.G. Wells's *The War of the Worlds,* have been played by regional orchestras. Mr. Nardo has written short stories, articles, textbooks, screenplays, and several teleplays, including an episode of ABC's "Spenser: For Hire." In addition, his screenplay *The Bet* won an award from the Massachusetts Artists Foundation. Mr. Nardo lives with his wife and son on Cape Cod, Massachusetts.

Picture Credits